"In this book, David Molian explores beautifully the nuances of family business and their importance to the global economy on so many levels, not least the jobs they provide, the wealth they create and the impact they have on communities too. It also provides a detailed look at the impact family firms have had over time and the increasingly global connectivity of family members in businesses today. There is also a good look at the impact that different generations are having, not just on the business but the wealth that they have created too, and the impact that it has had, and continues to have too.

The juxtaposition of history, historic events and the role of families over time is well documents and explored in this book that really does put the family business sector under the microscope, exploring its evolution and influence over time, the importance of certain places in groupings of wealthy families in business and the scale and reach of some of the biggest family firms around the world.

Geographical influences and differences are also explored in this comprehensive look at the world of family business with plenty of examples documented throughout. A challenging but comprehensive take on the sector which provides narrative, challenge and thought-provoking insights along the way.

Looking to the future and the likely 'tsunami of wealth' that will be transferred in the next few years is also looked at with respect, and the role of the next generation who want to do things differently, and the differing desires of the different generations involved in these businesses today.

This book is a great insight into the different aspects of family business to include legacy, philanthropy, the evolution of the role of women, geography and communication, historical context and influence and so much more besides.

In my opinion, a family business book that is positively different to any that I have seen before that is well worth a read by anyone with an interest in truly understanding and appreciating the essence of family business today, and how it has evolved over the years."

Paul Andrews, *Founder and CEO – Family Business United*

The Dynasty Effect

As the tech billionaires dominate the headlines, this groundbreaking book reveals the overlooked yet formidable influence of multi-generational family wealth on the global economy. It provides essential insights into the largest wealth transfer in human history – as 2% of the global population inherits vast fortunes over the next 25 years – revealing how this tsunami of inherited capital will transform investment landscapes, industrial financing, and potentially undermine nation-state autonomy.

Drawing from extensive research and industry expertise, David Molian charts the meteoric rise of ultra-wealthy dynasties whose collective impact rivals – and may outlast – Silicon Valley's tech titans. It charts the historical patterns behind industry-dominating family businesses and their evolution into business dynasties, and how the coming $30+ trillion wealth transfer will reshape global finance, investment, and economic development. In stagnating economic times, the search for growth and prosperity dominates government agendas throughout the world. The evidence suggests that family businesses outpace their peers. Through numerous case histories and industry analyses, this book explains why and how harnessing and supporting their success may be a critical part of regenerating national economies. It also explains the forces – chiefly the components of globalism – that have propelled family wealth in the eastern hemisphere in the last half-century.

Essential reading for anyone seeking to understand where true economic power lies in the 21st century, the book is specifically of interest to professionals involved in family business, including private banks, family offices, family consultants, law firms, and large accountancy practices.

David Molian has consulted with numerous multinational companies, including Unilever, Diageo, and Shell. For the last 25 years, he has focused on working with independent businesses, many of them family-owned, and has taught at Imperial College and Insead before joining Cranfield. He has worked with some of the UK's most outstanding growth success stories, including Cobra Beer, Hotel Chocolat, Belvoir Cordials, Thatcher's Cider, Pacific Direct, and Go Ape. He has provided commentary and opinion for *The Financial Times*, *Director Magazine*, *The Daily Telegraph*, *Fresh Business Thinking*, and many other publications, and has appeared on national and local television. He is a graduate of the University of Oxford and holds an MBA from Cranfield School of Management.

The Dynasty Effect

The Real Impact of Family Businesses on the Global Economy

David Molian

Routledge
Taylor & Francis Group
LONDON AND NEW YORK

Designed cover image: Getty Images – FotoMak

First published 2026
by Routledge
4 Park Square, Milton Park, Abingdon, Oxon OX14 4RN

and by Routledge
605 Third Avenue, New York, NY 10158

Routledge is an imprint of the Taylor & Francis Group, an informa business

British Library Cataloguing-in-Publication Data
A catalogue record for this book is available from the British Library

ISBN: 978-1-041-16620-7 (hbk)
ISBN: 978-1-041-15866-0 (pbk)
ISBN: 978-1-003-68548-7 (ebk)

DOI: 10.4324/9781003685487

Typeset in Goudy
by Newgen Publishing UK

To my children and their children

Contents

Preface

This book has been nearly 40 years in the making. That is not to imply that I am a very slow writer, though 1,000 usable words equals a good day's output. Rather, the seeds of this book were sown all the way back in 1975, in the nine months between leaving school and starting university. I had no idea of this at the time, of course, but like many things in one's life this particular interest – in family business – has come round full circle. Now in my 60s and with the benefit of the long view that advancing years bring, I can see that it is so.

In July of that year, I embarked on what was then a rite of passage for many school leavers: the Interrail trip. For a month and the princely sum of about £50 – I believe – a young person could spend his or her days riding the rails of Europe from Calais to Thessaloniki and Alicante to Aarhus. Night travel was included as well: in fact, if money was tight, overnight trains were one way of saving on accommodation. With the help of Thomas Cook's European train timetable, my travelling companion and I worked out an extreme variant of this for the really tight-fisted. If you wanted to spend a couple of days somewhere and save the price of a night in a youth hostel, you could catch a long-distance evening train leaving at, say, 11 at night, get off at a half-way point in the early hours, cross platforms, pick up a train travelling in the opposite direction and arrive back at your original point of departure in time to see the sunrise. All it required was the Cook's timetable, a reliable alarm clock, and the resilience of youth.

At the planning stage, I told my mother that I was intending to include Paris in my itinerary, and she suggested I look in on one of my great-aunts, on my father's side. She would appreciate a visit from a great-nephew, my mother said, and prior to my grandmother's death the two sisters had been close. So I wrote and duly received a warm reply, inviting me to visit. I had never met Dora before and knew only that she was the widow of a dealer in diamonds and other precious stones. Arriving in France, my pal Chris and I spent our first day in

Paris dutifully sightseeing and caught a late-night train from the Gare de Lyon. We left when the train stopped at Auxerre, I think, at some ungodly hour in the morning, hastily changed platforms and ten minutes later jumped aboard the train back to Paris.

Great-aunt Dora lived in grand style in an apartment on one of Paris's main boulevards close to the Champs Elysées. In preparation, I had been polishing my schoolboy French, but it was not needed: she seemed very happy to speak English. The morning passed in large part with her reminiscing of times spent with the extended family at my grandfather's house in St Raphaël, of which I had heard but knew little. "It was so lovely," she said. "He designed it himself, you know, the Villa Provençal." I hadn't the heart to mention that it had long since been demolished, to make way for a block of flats. "We had such delightful times there – your father, your uncle, and all the cousins. Your grandfather loved to entertain." Among the cousins were her own two children, of a similar age to my father.

As I listened to this gracious and elegant elderly lady recalling days on the beaches of the Côte d'Azur, it was hard to reconcile her life as it had become with the image in my mind of a small girl, standing on the quayside of Tilbury Docks beside her siblings, fresh off the boat from Danzig – now Gdansk – and carrying her worldly possessions in a small suitcase. My knowledge of family history was sketchy, but I knew that my father's family on his mother's side had arrived in Britain from Galicia in what is now southern Poland sometime around the start of the 20th century. My grandmother, Yetta, had gone on to found a small chain of couture shops in the West End, selling high fashion to high society: Dora had spent some years working with her husband on the great ocean liners that crossed the Atlantic between the wars, as jewellers of note to the rich and famous. The couple lived between London and Paris. In her widowhood, Dora had chosen Paris, and her children, the two cousins who had played with my father in the gardens of the Villa Provençal, had made their lives, respectively, in London and Paris. It was a life that certainly beat the penurious and precarious existence of a shtetl in an Austro-Hungarian province.

Dora's is a story shared by countless other emigrés who fled the poverty, repression, and general hopelessness of their lives in Poland, Moldova, Bessarabia, Russia and elsewhere in the eastern and middle European Jewish diaspora. Her history is unique only insofar as it is personal to me, my sister and my own family – her descendants. My father, curiously enough, took virtually no interest in his own family background and would say very little about his upbringing, even when pressed. I would go so far as to say that he rejected the slightly rootless cosmopolitanism embraced by the preceding generation in favour of a fierce assertion of his own British identity. I certainly learned more about my family history from those two hours or so chatting with Dora, which Chris, who was a forbearing sort of chap, listened to with a patient acquiescence.

At the end of the conversation, she asked about our travel plans. They were still vague. We intended to continue through Italy and Austria, through Yugoslavia as it then was, and on to Greece, before making our way back to England. Chris had an idea that he might visit friends of his family in Denmark, so at some point our paths would split. "Why don't you come back through France?" said Dora. "My daughter Anita and her husband have a place outside Chartres. They would love to meet you."

And so it was that three weeks later, I found myself in Vers-lès-Chartres, at the Abbaye de l'O, formerly a convent of a silent order of nuns. Dora's daughter Anita and her husband François spent summers there, away from the heat and traffic of Paris. Theirs was a love match, and an unusual example of a union between the two main branches of European Jewry: the Ashkenazis of central and eastern Europe, and the Sephardis of the Iberian Peninsula. They had met and married while still in their teens and spent their early life in North Africa, where François's career as a banker had taken him to Morocco. Anita had made a life in journalism, first as a columnist on teenage matters at *Elle*, and latterly as a gardening writer and designer. "When I turned 40," she told me, "I realised that my time writing for teenagers in a column called *Nous, les jeunes filles*, was definitely up. So I reinvented myself as a writer about gardening and then as a *paysagiste*, a landscape architect, and garden designer." She had remarkable drive and energy. Most evenings, after dinner, she spent two hours writing fiction as well.

François had led no less an interesting life as both banker and industrialist. When I first met him, he was President of the European subsidiary of the US oilfields construction company, Brown & Root. He was a handsome and charming man, what the French call *un vrai monsieur*, a real gent. His English was immaculate, although spoken with a slight nasal twang which seemed at odds with his urbane comportment. "You will have to excuse my London accent," he said as we sat around the pool. "My British nanny was a cockney."

He was also a scion of one of the great Jewish 19th-century dynasties that had arisen during France's Second Empire, the Pereires, originally Pereiras, of Portuguese descent. His ancestors, Emile and Isaac, were beneficiaries of the emancipation of Jews after the French Revolution and seized the opportunity that was created with both hands. Arriving in Paris in the early 1820s from Bordeaux, the brothers set about creating a banking and industrial empire with ferocious energy. They were behind France's first railway, from central Paris to St Germain, and constructed the Gare Saint-Lazare. Within two decades, their railway interests grew to encompass much of the rest of France, and large parts of Spain and Austria. They built and operated a transatlantic liner company, installed gas services and established the first bus company in Paris, developed real estate and insurance businesses, created the holiday resort of Arcachon north of Bordeaux and set up the Crédit Mobilier, an investment bank to compete with the French house of Rothschild. A full list of their commercial interests would occupy another page. In short, their endeavours made them enormously rich.

It didn't last. With the collapse of that frenzied era of entrepreneurial capitalism, so vividly chronicled by Emile Zola, so did the family's business fortunes. They overextended themselves and were opposed by the Banque de France in their attempt to challenge the Banque's monopoly on issuing currency. Victims, perhaps, of an excessive belief in their own publicity and of competition from rivals, they saw their empire crumble and then dissipate. Much was absorbed by the French state and other national governments. Some of their businesses ceased to be viable. The family's grand townhouse in the Faubourg St Honoré is now the British Embassy, and the headquarters of the Crédit Mobilier is today the Ritz Hotel. In a final humiliation, their great country house at Gretz-Armainvilliers, served by its own railway station, was bombed by mistake by the US Air Force in the Second World War. Their name is remembered in Paris's Boulevard Pereire and the metro station of the same name in the 17th arrondissement – much of which they developed – and in the odd plaque and name place in Bordeaux.

Emile and Isaac's descendants were still wealthy by anyone's standards and moved in the upper ranks of French society. They intermarried with the other prominent Jewish families: one of François's grandmothers was a Rothschild (clearly the families had patched things up), and he had served on the board of the Rothschild family bank in Paris. But things were never the same again.

I met Anita and François on several further occasions, both at their country home and in London. They were kind enough to share more of the family history, much of which was recorded in photograph albums, engravings, and portraits. I was then caught up in my own career, and contact ceased. The next I heard was that François had died, sadly prematurely, of leukaemia. Anita was to outlive him for many years and died in New York at the age of 102. Their son Marc, whom I knew slightly, was a highly successful fund manager cum banker, founder of his own firm, who made his career in London.

On my father's side of the family, there is a strong tradition of first-generation entrepreneurship, but no enduring business legacy. In the case of my grandfather, I know exactly what prevented that: his factories in Germany and

Austria were confiscated in the 1930s by the Nazis in their mass expropriation of businesses owned by Jews. In his 50s, he was obliged to end his idyllic life in St Raphaël and returned to England to start again. He chose to open an antiques shop in Torquay, thus exchanging the French Riviera for what the marketing department of the Great Western Railway optimistically branded the English Riviera. He also died relatively young and left his estate to my grandmother, whose instinct for business deserted her in later life in a series of bad property investments. There was no family business – or family fortune come to that – left to inherit.

In the first part of my adult life, I spent some time as a freelance writer, business founder, and co-owner before switching in the latter part to teach and mentor budding and actual entrepreneurs at business schools in Britain and France. Unquestionably, I was better suited to the advising than the doing – being off the pitch rather than on it, though still closely involved in the game. A large number of the entrepreneurs I taught or mentored were members of family businesses: in some cases, husband and wife couples who had founded a firm which they intended to pass on to their children, but in most instances the descendants of the original founders, the second or third generation family members. Contrasting their story with my own, I wondered from time to time what my life would have been like had my forbears bequeathed a business, and my sister and I had found ourselves in their shoes. In my 40s, I was invited to join the Advisory Board of one of the country's leading family business consultancies and served for two years on the panel of judges awarding the Coutts (Bank) Family Business Prize. This turned out to be the most fabulous opportunity to meet a diverse range of family business members, not merely second or third generation, but descendants in their fifth, sixth generation, and even beyond. But it was only ever an adjunct to the day job, which was designing and directing development programmes for first-generation business founders and their teams of senior managers.

Now in retirement, theoretically at least, I have the time and space in which to reflect more deeply on the questions that have long been at the back of my mind, questions that sit on a broader canvas. What ensures the longevity of a family business so that it continues through the generations? Are the factors which contribute to that longevity all of equal significance, or are some of greater importance than others? Do some environments provide more fertile conditions than others to support the continuity of family businesses? Is it always a good thing that a family business should endure, or are there times when it makes better sense for the business on which a family has built its fortunes to pass, wholly or partly, into the hands of others? Concomitantly, at what point does the family business transform itself into the business family?[1]

Are there moments in history – like that of the Industrial Revolution in Britain, the French Second Empire, the rise of China, the growing wealth of the Middle East or the new dynamism of South Asia – that favour the creation and economic heft of family businesses? And, perhaps most intriguingly of all, are we ourselves living through a time in which both the dominance and the composition of family businesses are shifting irrevocably across the globe?

In this book, I do my best to address these questions and others, and to answer them as far as I can. I should, perhaps, add that between the writing of this book and its publication, events will occur that make some of the information contained in it out of date. Despite the temptation to edit endlessly, every manuscript needs a deadline, and the modern world moves at an ever-increasing pace.

Note

1 A business family is one which is bound together by its collective investments, rather than by a focus on a single, family-controlled/managed enterprise.

Acknowledgements

I would like to record my thanks to all those who have played their part in sparking my interest in family businesses, and in bringing this book to publication:

First, to all the many family business owners I have come into contact with over the years, who have shared their experience and wisdom: they are too many to list, but I hope they will recognise the part they have played in shaping my thinking.

Second, and specifically, to those current and former members of Coutts and Weatherbys private banks, who provided the opportunities and introductions that furthered my education in this topic.

Third, to those contributors to the case studies featured in the book, who were kind enough to give their time and to offer their insights.

Fourth, to my eldest daughter, Sabina Borton, co-founder of ESB Consulting, for her help with Chapter 3 of this book.

Fifth, to the team at Routledge, ever-helpful and supportive.

Sixth, to my second cousin, Roger Winfield, Blaustein family historian, who has graciously shared both the fruits of his research and his base of contacts.

Any errors of fact are my own, as are the conclusions and opinions expressed in this book.

Introduction

Whether we like it or not, we are all members of a family through the fact – or accident – of birth. It has been said that you should choose your parents wisely. Alas, that option is not yet available. From our earliest days, we have to play the genetic hand that we are dealt and make the best of the circumstances in which we find ourselves.

The family is arguably the fundamental basis on which all human societies are built. Over the years, there have been various attempts to suppress or destroy it, usually in the name of some ideological goal: the collectivisation of Soviet peasant farms under Stalin, for instance, Mao's abortive Great Leap Forward between 1958 and 1962, or the madness of Cambodia's Khmer Rouge under Pol Pot in the 1970s. Most recently, we have seen the callous abduction of Ukrainian children in an attempt at the "Russification" of the next generation. All such acts eventually fail to achieve their ends, albeit at the cost of millions of lives, economic catastrophe, and social turmoil. Sooner or later, the family reasserts itself as the primary unit of social and economic cohesion.

With luck, humanity has learned the lessons of these disastrous experiments, and they will not be endlessly repeated. In the modern era, our major concern is rather that families are not replacing themselves at a sustainable rate, and that population levels in advanced economies are maintained only through immigration. Rich countries are simply not having enough children, despite the best endeavours of the Mormon inhabitants of Utah. In developed economies, an average replacement rate of at least 2.1 children per couple is necessary to maintain a stable population, and no Western European country has met that target this century. The reasons for this are many and complex: it is enough to say here that the more affluent a society becomes, the lower is the corresponding rate of infant mortality, the greater the average citizen's lifespan, fewer children are born to the rising generation, and women start their families later in life. Affluent economies have extensive welfare provision, and we as

DOI: 10.4324/9781003685487-1

parents no longer need multiple children of working age to support us, at least financially, in our old age.

That said, if the projections are correct and unless something changes dramatically, the rich nations of the world are facing a demographic time bomb. The ticking is growing progressively louder from the middle of this century onwards. An ever-expanding population of elderly people will be supported by a shrinking number of those who are economically active. It gets worse. Some of those who study global demographics predict that the world population as a whole will not only cease to grow but actually go into reverse, as the poorer south catches up with the richer north and adopts the same trend of having fewer children. An article in the *Financial Times* on Wednesday, 29 January 2025, reports that by the end of this century, according to the United Nations, no country will have a birth rate exceeding 2.3.

To many of you reading this book, this may not come as news: these facts and predictions have been widely publicised in recent years. I draw attention to them because, first, they set the scene and, second, they serve to underscore the significance of the family, and more specifically the family business, in the minds of more enlightened politicians and public policymakers. The health and prosperity of economies across the world is closely tied to the health and prosperity of family businesses, and this fact, I would suggest, is widely unacknowledged and under-appreciated. The continuing success of family businesses, as I set out to show, is critical to navigating our way through the very significant social, economic, and political challenges of our own times, and those that lie ahead. By way of illustration, the Family Business Research Foundation,[1] an arm of Family Business UK which lobbies for family enterprises, maintains that over 90% of private businesses in Britain are family-managed and/or controlled. All told, they turn over £1.7 trillion, equating to roughly half the country's GDP [gross domestic product: essentially the nation's annual wealth], and employ almost 14 million people.

* * *

We are fascinated by families. As individuals, we spend much of our lives dealing with the demands of parental expectations, managing our relations with siblings and spouses, and attempting to be the best parents and grandparents we can be. In many families, there is a keeper of the family history who takes on the task of chronicling the lines of descent and maintaining a repository of anecdotes and events that would otherwise pass out of memory. Royal and noble families employ professional archivists, such is the wealth of material to be conserved and the interests of historians and genealogists to be accommodated. As the generations increase, the task expands. Family histories, both mythical and actual, have formed the basis of dramatic retelling since the Greek tragedian

Aeschylus described the downfall of the house of Atreus at the hands of the gods. In modern times, millions follow the fictional story of the Roy family in the TV drama *Succession* and the dramatised tribulations of the real-life Gettys and the Guccis. There is perhaps comfort to be found in the knowledge that all the money in the world cannot prevent bust-ups, rivalries, estrangements, and tragic loss. The American writer Scott Fitzgerald allegedly remarked to Ernest Hemingway that the rich are different from you and me, to which Hemingway replied yes, they have more money. In other respects, they are much the same, merely actors on a bigger set. Even academics have succumbed to this fascination with the rich and how they spend their money.[2]

In the course of examining the role and significance of family businesses, we touch inevitably on the psychodrama. The dynamics of family relationships add an extra layer of complexity to the challenges of managing and sustaining a business and the creation of wealth. The central focus of this book, however, is the significance of the family business in the global economy, the wealth that arises from these enterprises, and the geographic shifts in family influence of recent years. The reports, surveys, and listings which address this topic all start from the same point of departure: the majority of enterprises across the world *are family businesses*. The percentages may differ for individual countries, but the pattern is consistent across developed and developing economies. On reflection, this should maybe come as little surprise. If the basic economic unit of human society is the family, then we should expect a more than healthy representation of families as economic actors. More to the point, our window onto the present is partly shaped by what could be termed "dynastic overhang": the family businesses that populate the landscape today are in many cases multi-generational enterprises. To take one prominent example, the British Royal Family, which is in the business of constitutional monarchy and commonly refers to itself as *The Firm*, can trace its lineage – and legitimacy – back over more than 1,000 years. The family is the most enduring of social structures. Empires collapse, kingdoms come and go, nation-states succumb to invasion, and tribes wax and wane in their affiliations. But families persist across time and space.

Il Faut Cultiver Notre Jardin*

Iford Manor close to Bath is approached by a narrow, winding road, bordered by hedges on either side. After what seems like an age, but is actually little over half a mile, a small yet ornate bridge, the house, and its surrounding buildings come into view. The first time you see it, your breath is taken away. It is an enchanting vista. The manor is not a grand house in the style of, say, nearby Longleat, but it is perfectly proportioned in the Georgian mode. To one side are the exquisitely converted outbuildings that now comprise the café and restaurant, and behind rise the celebrated gardens, in a series of steep terraces. You are deep in the southernmost valley of the Cotswolds, that rolling landscape which extends down from Gloucestershire into north Wiltshire and Somerset. On a fine summer's day, Iford is the embodiment of the English countryside of the imagination.

The current custodians of the house and the surrounding estate are William and Marianne Cartwright-Hignett, the second generation of the family to reside there. In 1965, William's mother purchased the estate from the nephew of the celebrated garden designer Harold Peto, who created Iford's garden largely in the Mediterranean style and populated it with classical statuary and places for repose and reflection. Elizabeth Cartwright's primary interest was in farming, and over time she consolidated the adjoining farms into what is now an 850-acre estate. In partnership with her husband, John Hignett (a dairy farmer), she turned her attention to restoring the gardens, which had fallen into disrepair. William and Marianne took over the management of Iford in 2016 and have put their own, very distinctive stamp on it.

"My mother handed this over to us right after we married," says William. "I had always known that, as the only child, caring for Iford would fall to me – I might otherwise have become a barrister or a diplomat. But we embraced the opportunity to build on what my mother had achieved. In fact, there was really little choice. For Iford to flourish, we needed to expand it as a commercial concern. Maintaining the gardens and heritage alone requires hundreds of thousands of pounds annually, and we have a passion to keep it going as well as an obligation to share this wonderful place, which has been open to the public for over a century. Growth gives you options."

In collaboration with a neighbour, a cider-making operation using the estate's surplus apples had started in 2015, the first vintage appearing the following year for the couple's wedding. Then came the café and the restaurant, which this year [2025] won Best Newcomer in the Trencherman's Awards. The acquisition of two local pubs is in progress, and the estate has renovated cottages as holiday lets. An arts festival, started by Elizabeth, had outgrown the venue by 2018, but William and Marianne inaugurated the summer Iford Jazz festival during the pandemic, which continues to sell out. Annual visitor footfall to the valley, the couple estimate, is roughly 70,000 – in fact, to protect the heritage and maintain the atmosphere of peaceful repose, the numbers are limited within the garden itself to just 20,000 a year.

What makes their enterprise specifically a family concern? "Only when I married Marianne would I describe Iford as a true family business," says William – and Marianne brought with her a high-flying City career in private equity as a tax specialist, which has greatly strengthened Iford's commercial firepower. "I think it's passion sustained over a generational cycle which truly distinguishes a family business," William maintains. "We don't have a plan so much as a mission, which is to sustain this amazing place for the long-term with the help of a wonderful team and the wider community. While the passion persists across generations, it assumes a different form for each generation. For my parents, it was farming, the garden, the landscape. For us, it started with the garden and heritage and has broadened out into hospitality, jazz and wider community engagement. I think that every so often a family business needs rejuvenating as well as having periods of stability."

The couple have two small children under 10. I asked about their intentions for the next generation, and they were adamant that their offspring must pursue their own paths. At the same time, they would clearly be delighted if at least one of the boys were to choose to follow in their footsteps. "At William's 42nd birthday party," Marianne tells me, "Our elder boy said that when his father reached his next birthday and became very old, it would be fine because he would be able to help him. It was very touching!"

If you're obliged to live over the shop – and William points out that despite keeping the manor as a family home, they live more or less *in* the shop – it's a very nice place in which to do it.

*Voltaire, *Candide*. [We must cultivate our garden]

Source: In conversation with the author.

What Is a Family – and, by Extension, What Counts as a Family Business?

The answer to the first question was altogether simpler in past decades. The *basic* family unit was defined very largely by marriage and a lifespan that embraced the three generations of parents, grandparents and children. The *extended* family was defined by blood and, to a great degree, by the closeness of relationships between cousins, aunts/uncles, nieces/nephews, and so forth. In societies where kinship is highly prized, such as among the clans of Scotland and its English-speaking diaspora, those bonds and links were and are tighter; in more atomised societies, they are looser.

In the 21st century, families take on a more diverse character: we have so-called traditional, one-parent, "blended" in the form of step-parents and step-children, parents of the same sex, divorced parents maintaining separate households, and so on. The picture is complicated, and likely to stay that way. In Saudi Arabia, the ruling family of Saud reportedly comprises at least 15,000 living members and maybe more, depending on how you count the numerous siblings, half-siblings, first cousins, distant cousins, and so forth. Defining what it is to count as a *family business* is also not straightforward. Is it enough to qualify if you are a first-generation husband and wife team, or does the enterprise only become a "real" family business if the next generation actively participates as employees or shareholders? Following the definition established by the European Commission, the European Family Businesses Association[3] maintains that a business is to be considered a family business if:

- The majority of decision-making rights are in the possession of the natural person(s) who established the firm, or in the possession of the natural person(s) who has/have acquired the share capital of the firm, or in the possession of their spouses, parents, child or children's direct heirs.
- The majority of decision-making rights are indirect or direct.
- At least one representative of the family or kin is formally involved in the governance of the firm.

And when it comes to public [listed] companies, the qualification is:

- Listed companies meet the definition of family enterprise if the person who established or acquired the firm (share capital) or their families or descendants possess 25% of the decision-making rights mandated by their share capital.

It's a pretty wide definition, and unsurprisingly the European Commission asserts that over 60% of businesses across Europe are family businesses, and that they range from sole proprietorships to large multinationals. Clearly, the broader the definition, the greater the number of businesses that will be caught in the net. The same claim, that family businesses comprise more than half the business population, features in surveys of numerous countries outside Europe, produced by publications such as *Tharawat* and by public agencies responsible for data collection. According to the US Bureau of the Census, for instance, 90% of American businesses are family-owned or -controlled, and the same applies to around one-third of the businesses in the Fortune 500.[4] Walmart, founded in 1962, is valued at the time of writing at over US$600 billion and is the world's largest company by revenue. Although listed on the New York Stock Exchange, the business is still effectively controlled by the Walton family, who own 48.9%[5] of the corporation and occupy senior positions in the company. The company's revenues are almost twice those of the next on the list, Berkshire Hathaway, the business founded and still controlled by Warren Buffett and family. The Buffett family are also minority shareholders in their company, but the share structure gives them control. If you can afford it, you can buy shares in Berkshire Hathaway [at around $480 per B share], but Warren Buffett can outvote you by a factor of 10,000 per share.

The next generation of the Buffett family sits on Berkshire Hathaway's board, and the second and third generations of the Waltons are involved in Walmart. It might be arguable whether a "real" family business has to be a multi-generational one, but family succession at least shows that the business has passed the test of time. It's no easy task. Data from the US tells us that 30% of families survive the transition from first to second generation, and only 13% make the transition from second to third.[6] Four per cent make it to the fourth generation, and apparently so few survive to the fifth that no reliable data is available.[7] [Given that the US is still a relatively young country, the last fact is perhaps not surprising.] Head-hunter Russell Reynolds Associates' 2019 *Pan-European Report on Family-Owned Business* is slightly more encouraging, but reports the same pattern of steep decline from one generation to the next. The reasons for this will be explored later in this book.

A Case Study in Failure

Many other countries have their own version of the [British] English saying "clogs to clogs in three generations." The American variant is "from shirtsleeves to shirtsleeves," and the French "sabots aux sabots[8] en trois générations." The moral is universal: the first generation rises from humble origins to make money, the second lives off it, and the third dissipates what is left. There is even research evidence to suggest that this is a generalisable pattern,[9] although it flies in the face of much contrary evidence to say that extinction is inevitable. One recent example of third-generation failure familiar to British readers is the collapse of the retail chain Wilko [formerly Wilkinson]. The company was founded in Leicester as a hardware store in 1930 by James Kemsey Wilkinson and carried on by his son, Anthony, known as Tony. He was succeeded by his daughter Lisa and niece, Karin Swann. In 2014, Swann sold her 50% holding in the business to Lisa [in hindsight, a smart move], leaving Tony, his wife Christine, and Lisa the sole owners of the company. Third-generation Lisa assumed the role of chairman. At the time of its collapse in August 2023, Wilko was still wholly owned and managed by the Wilkinson family, with a workforce of 12,500 and 408 stores across the UK. While bad news for the employees, this debacle did not spell financial disaster to the Wilkinson clan: between 2013 and 2023, the family reportedly paid themselves £77 million in dividends. When called to account for the firm's insolvency, Lisa Wilkinson was given a distinctly hostile reception by Members of Parliament, accused by one of "burgling a failing business."[10]

It is hard not to conclude that in the Wilkinson case third-generation family wealth was created at the expense of destroying the value of the family business. This family can certainly afford a superior sort of clog. Perhaps a disastrous combination of avarice and managerial incompetence played a major role – certainly Wilko was noteworthy for its lack of professional, non-family business expertise at board level, unusual in a third-generation family business. The case is exceptional in other ways. It is far more common for family firms to fail or reconfigure themselves because of internal disputes between members. In fact, family concerns are well-known for their conservative approach to finance, reluctance to take on excessive debt and a tendency to reinvest heavily in their businesses. Critical to growing the prosperity of both the family *and* the business is an understanding of what Warren Buffett famously termed the snowball effect of cumulative interest.

At this point, it is worth invoking the Rule of 72.

Accumulation of Wealth and the Rule of 72

Had I been taught the Rule of 72 in my school maths classes, instead of the solving – or abject failure to solve – of quadratic equations, I might well be considerably richer. The principle is simple: the large effect of small numbers compounding over time. To many people [and I include myself], this is, however, not intuitive.

The Rule of 72 was first brought to wider public attention in 1494 when the Italian mathematician Luca Pacioli referred to it in his book on mathematics, *Summa de Arithmetica.*[11] It is a rule in the sense of being a rule of thumb. It applies to anything that grows at a compounded rate, such as national income, and predicts the future date at which a given quantity will double in value over time. You apply it by simple division. Thus:

> If the annual rate of growth is 5%, the initial quantity will double in *14.4* years [72/5]
> If the annual rate of growth is *10%*, the initial quantity will double in *7.2* years [72/10]

To illustrate: a starting sum of 100 on day 1 if compounded at an average annual rate of 5% becomes 105 on day 365, 110.25 [= 105 multiplied by 1.05] on day 730, and so on [with adjustments for leap years]. Assuming this continues with no changes, nearly halfway through year 14, that 100 has magically transformed itself into 200. More to the point, if during that period you were to *add to* that initial sum, you would double your money sooner. You simply need patience and what psychologists call "delayed gratification," i.e. resistance to the temptation to blow surplus money on enticing goodies like fancy cars and expensive holidays.

Of course, this example ignores the effects of inflation over time, which erodes the purchasing power of your gains, and the capacity of governments to tax wealth. Both affect the end result. But conversely the example also illustrates the desirability of a stable currency and moderate taxation policies if a democratically elected government wants its electorate to grow richer and vote for them next time around.

The formula is an approximation, but accurate enough for most purposes.[12] So if you think that whether an economy grows on average by 1% per annum or by 2% is an obscure matter best left to economists and policy wonks, think again. It really matters. At a growth rate of 1%, it takes 72 years for a country's national wealth – and, all other things being equal, its citizens' standard of living – to double. At a growth rate of 2%, that number halves to 36 years. When the Chinese economy was regularly growing at 7%, China's national wealth could be expected to double in a little over ten years. Perhaps most importantly the *average change in wealth per household* will be noticeably impacted by big variations in the size of national populations. If, like the United Kingdom in the years 2022–2024, you see a vicious combination of high inflation, continued low growth and a rapid rise in population numbers, people will justifiably feel poorer.

Let's turn from the macro to the micro. The UK government introduced a tax-free savings scheme called the Individual Savings Allowance [ISA] in April 1999. In simple terms, a British taxpayer was able to invest up to £10,000 every year, free of tax, the sum being split between stocks and shares and cash. There was a wide element of discretion – you could deposit the money in managed funds or choose your own allocation. However, the money was to be saved for the long term, and the scheme – and its subsequent variations – was essentially designed for the purposes of retirement: early withdrawals were subject to penalties.

The ISA allowance went up as time progressed. As I write, it is £20,000 per annum. In March 2024, wealth managers RBC Brewin Dolphin revealed that the top 25 ISA savers had achieved, on average, a fund value of £11.7 million, with no liability for tax.

To achieve this level of success, you needed:

- to be an astute investor
- to devote a lot of time to your portfolio
- to maximise your annual tax-free contributions [and have the cash available to do so]; you added more snow to the snowball as it rolled
- to put long-term goals ahead of short-term gratification
- and, more than anything, to understand the impact of compounding interest!

My firm belief is that an orientation towards the long term, plus strong numeracy, are also what underpin the longevity of successful multi-generational family businesses. On their own, these two factors are not enough: the business needs to adapt to changes in the marketplace, to be resilient in the face of external shocks like war, and to be able to preserve harmonious family relationships and inter-generational transfers of authority and ownership. These topics form a continuous thread within this book.

Organisation of this Book

This book is organised into four chapters.

Chapter 1, "The Family Through History," is a broad sweep through time, principally through Western history, which surveys the roles played in society by families over the ages. The West benefits from the enormous legacy of Roman law and custom, which did much to protect the status and legacies of families and their assets. Societies that were rigidly hierarchical gradually transformed themselves into looser structures in which social mobility was more easily attained, and family wealth was no longer the preserve of a privileged caste. This chapter examines the personal, social, economic and technological factors that propelled families into prominence and created fortunes. The tradition of family philanthropy also arose as many of those who have made great fortunes feel obligated to alleviate the conditions of the poor. This part also explores who wins and who loses in societies that are more fluid.

Chapter 2, "The Global Shift in the 20th and 21st Centuries," surveys the current status of family businesses worldwide and specifically the growing significance of the ultra-rich in the global economy. Today's ultra-wealthy families are effectively world citizens. It is no secret that wealth is concentrated in relatively few hands, but less well understood is the modern dominance of families whose wealth derives ultimately from their business interests. This chapter delves into the origin of that wealth, its geographical distribution and the progressive shift from West to East with the rise of Asia-Pacific, India, and the Middle East. Much of that shift results from the trends towards globalisation of the last half-century. The contributing factors of globalisation are dissected, as are the ways that family businesses have taken advantage of new trends in world trade. As part of this transformation, the presence of European families in the ranks of the ultra-rich has been diluted, although the dominance of North America remains uniquely strong.

Chapter 3, "The Social Network: The System That Preserves and Grows Family Wealth," is dedicated to the eco-system of support that wealthy families enjoy. That network divides between those who provide the support to their businesses and other assets that families control, and those who supply services to families in a private capacity. On the business side are banks and other professional advisors and, increasingly, the private wealth management offices which have expanded in line with the rise of the globally wealthy. On the private side are concierge services, private members' clubs, property search agencies, early years' childcare providers and elite schools and colleges. Their number has also risen exponentially as the demand for their services has risen inexorably. This chapter also examines where ultra-high net worth families choose to locate themselves, and their concentration in specific locations. A fictional case study charts the rise of a family business over three generations, to capture how the use of these networks grows and changes over time, as the rising generation enters the ranks of the globally wealthy.

Chapter 4, "The Tsunami of Wealth: More Money Than the World Has Ever Seen," probes the near-term impact of transferred family wealth. In the next two decades, trillions of dollars will flow between generations in the form of family inheritance. This cascade of wealth is unprecedented, and it will have an enormous impact not only on those who inherit but on the good causes that will benefit from their philanthropy and on public policymakers. This chapter delineates the differences that characterise the various generations, from Baby Boomers through to Generation Z, and explores how the attitudes of the beneficiaries are likely to change in comparison with their parents' beliefs: not merely in how they consume and the causes that they support, but in how they choose to invest and manage their wealth. National governments are already having to confront the challenge of the hyper-mobile, hyper-wealthy, and in many cases have yet to formulate policies that are not inherently contradictory. How will Europe in particular come to terms with this new breed of the super-rich?

Afterword

The bulk of this manuscript was drafted during 2024, prior to the election of Donald Trump as the 47th President of the United States of America. In a few short months, his presidency has laid down a gauntlet to the existing political and economic world order. He has said what was previously unsayable and taken mainstream orthodoxies head-on. Whether he means what he says or whether there is method in what many have called out as madness, history will judge. What cannot be disputed is that the "global settlement," in which the United States positioned itself as the guarantor of liberal democracy of last resort, can no longer be taken as read – and with it the globalisation that has powered the accumulation of so much family wealth. This concluding section, then, reflects on the implications for the subjects of this book: is this rupture in the world order a crisis or a new set of opportunities in disguise, which the agile will exploit to their advantage?

* * *

On a final note, I should make it clear that this book is not intended as a comprehensive history of the family business. No doubt there is an opportunity for one to be written, but there are others better qualified than I am to author it. This book is written from the perspective of one who has encountered many family businesses over the years, in both an academic and a commercial context, almost exclusively within a Western European environment. I have little to say about family businesses in Africa, Latin America, Oceania [the Pacific islands], or Australasia: not because they are insignificant in their regional economies. They are, and very much so. But they have yet to make a substantial impact on the global economy, and have little prospect of doing so in the near-term, as the data which I draw on in later chapters of this book illustrate. All the same, the book is written in the spirit of explaining what makes family businesses tick, sharing insights into what contributes to their successes [and setbacks] and, above all, providing encouragement to keep going when the going gets tough.

Notes

1 See www.fbrf.org.uk/reports
2 See, for instance, *Handbook on Wealth and the Super-Rich*, Edward Elgar, 2016.
3 The European umbrella body for national family business associations.
4 As of 23 April 2024.
5 Source: Global Family Business Index, 2023.
6 SCORE website.

7 www.thisiscapitalism.org
8 "Clogs to clogs."
9 Clogs to Clogs in Three Generations? Explaining Entrepreneurial Performance in Britain Since 1850. Tom Nicholas, *Journal of Economic History*, vol 59, issue 3, published online by Cambridge University Press, 3 March 2009.
10 View the televised interview at www.dailymotion.com/video/x8q25w0
11 It is unclear whether Pacioli discovered the Rule or just publicised it.
12 You can modify the number 72 to account for calculating the doubling effect of growth month by month, for example.

Further Reading

No One Left: Why the World Needs More Children, Morland, Paul, Swift Press, 2025.

The Snowball: Warren Buffett and the Business of Life, Schroeder, Alice, Bloomsbury Publishing, 2009.

Business Families and Family Businesses, 3rd edition, Globe Law and Business, 2025.

1
The Family through History

The Story of Dr Wu

The second half of my professional life was spent as academic faculty, on the staff of business schools in Britain and France. The job of a business school faculty member divides more or less into three parts: you teach, you conduct research, and, inevitably, you deal with a certain amount of admin.

My research interest was primarily in developing case studies for teaching. At some point, around the mid-2000s, it struck me that the UK business school where I was teaching badly lacked materials about Chinese businesses at a time when China was clearly becoming a major force in the global economy. By happy coincidence, a team of student MBAs was working on a project for a Chinese entrepreneur. I met them, and it turned out that the entrepreneur in question was due to visit the campus shortly. I arranged to spend some time with him, to hear his story. Let us call him Dr Wu.

Dr Wu turned out to be a slightly built, self-effacing man in middle-age. His life began in rural China, far from any major city, and in his very early childhood his family had lived with the consequences of Mao's disastrous Great Leap Forward. "For two years we had almost nothing to eat," he told me. "At one stage, we were eating grass. That was all there was." Dr Wu was one of the few lucky ones. His potential was identified early on, and he was fast-tracked for academic success. On leaving school, he was first sent for training at a Chinese university linked to a teaching hospital. Having qualified as a doctor, he was then dispatched as one of a handful of graduates to the West, for post-graduate training in London, where he specialised in haematology. While he worked his way up to becoming a Registrar, he enrolled at the same time at my business school for a part-time MBA at weekends. Dr Wu had already conceived a plan for a new business venture to be launched back in China. He just needed to acquire the skills and knowledge to start his own firm.

DOI: 10.4324/9781003685487-2

All this was taking place in the 1990s. By the time we met a decade later, Dr Wu was married with his own family. They lived in north London, where his sons attended a prestigious private school. Wu divided his time between the UK and China, where he had created a business in the special economic zone bordering Hong Kong. His company manufactured haemodialysis equipment – essentially blood purification kits – and was heavily oriented towards export markets in the West. The project on which the MBA team was working was an analysis of how and where to expand the firm internationally. Dr Wu had serious ambitions. In time, he explained to me, he hoped that his sons would also train in medicine in Britain, and would take over the firm for the next generation. "Family is very important to Chinese people," he told me. "We think long term. I want to hand over a successful business to my sons when they are ready."

This modest, quietly spoken man is one of the most impressive people I have ever met. It was only *after* our meeting that I began to understand fully the scale of his achievements and contrast them with my own comparatively easy ride through life. His life's journey compressed within a single lifetime several centuries of Western history, from agrarian to Industrial Revolution through to the globalisation of medical technology – and he was barely 50! He prefers to remain anonymous, and I shall respect his wishes, saying only that he has become extremely successful. In the person of one individual is embodied the powerhouse that is modern China.

The Family through History

Strictly speaking, human history is what can be known about the past by virtue of written records.[1] We can trace these back about 5,000 years to Egyptian hieroglyphics and Sumerian cuneiform writings from the Middle East. These chronicle the reigns of monarchs and significant events such as battles, but yield little insight into the lives of the ruling classes. The Old Testament of the Bible is more recent, being composed over many centuries between about 1200 and 165 BC, and amid the accounts of the tribes and tribulations of Israel it details episodes of family life such as the disputes between the Houses of Judah and Saul. The earliest Greek historian of the first millennium BC, Herodotus, delighted in collecting curious anecdotes, while his partial contemporary, Thucydides, was concerned with covering the war between Athens and Sparta in the 5th century BC. Not until the Roman era do we find primarily biographical historians – principally Plutarch, Suetonius, and Tacitus – whose focus is on the personalities who shaped events and, by extension, the families from which they sprang.

During the early history of the Roman Republic, power and wealth were concentrated in the ranks of a relatively small group of aristocratic families, the patrician class.[2] They enjoyed inherited political privileges and provided military as well as political leadership. Beneath them was the broader body of citizens, the plebs, a term that needs no translation, and sandwiched between the patricians and the plebs were the *equites* or knights, roughly speaking, a prosperous bourgeois class of property-owning families. Much of Roman Republican history consists of power struggles between these three "orders" or social classes. The Republican era ended when Rome's territorial expansion outstripped the capacity of the existing system of government, Octavian defeated Marc Antony at the battle of Actium, and the victor proclaimed himself *princeps* – or emperor. The Roman Empire was underway. Octavian, known thereafter as Augustus, was the great-nephew of Julius Caesar and founder of the imperial Julio-Claudian dynasty. The period from 27 BC to 68 AD, when this family dominated the Roman world, is the first well-documented dynastic psychodrama of Western civilisation, from which Robert Graves drew inspiration for his award-winning novel *I, Claudius*.

Between them, the three historians mentioned above provide biographies of the Julio-Claudian dynasty and some of the emperors who succeeded the bloodline after the suicide of Nero in 68 AD. The Julio-Claudian family business was in effect the rule of the empire, and the business endured across five generations [including Julius Caesar himself]. The line of succession was largely oblique. Claudius, for example, was the great-nephew of Tiberius, who was an adopted heir and stepson to Augustus as the product of Augustus's wife's first marriage. Last in the Imperial line, Nero, was from a separate, collateral branch of the clan entirely. Palace intrigue, rivalries, betrayals, and scandal yielded rich material for the biographers whose accounts read at times more like salacious gossip columns. It is implied, if not actually stated in explicit judgements, that the family's eventual downfall was thanks to decadence and the dissolute nature of their lifestyles.

The extravagance and luxurious living portrayed were funded by wealth primarily accumulated from property and land-holdings, a share of the spoils of Imperial conquest, and taxation that was directed into the Imperial fiscus, or treasury. The distinction between what was owned by the state and owned by the family was a hazy one. The patrician class, of which these early emperors were a part, possessed extensive land-holdings across Italy and a portfolio of properties within Rome itself. Estates yielded agricultural produce, whose surplus could be sold, and property produced rents. In a pre-industrial[3] society, the shortest route to accumulating vast amounts of wealth was through class privilege and patronage, and thereby holding on to it. "Tax-farming," the possession of exclusive territorial licences to collect taxes on behalf of the Imperial Treasury, afforded a well-known chance to build fortunes. The steady rate of urbanisation during the late Republican and Imperial periods also created opportunities to make serious money. Rome was for centuries the most populous city on earth, and at its largest the number of inhabitants is estimated at 1 million. The principal city of Roman Gaul, Lyon, attained a population of 50,000, and London 30,000. Roman civil and cultural life centred on city-dwelling, and urban populations needed daily feeding and fresh water supplies. Rome itself depended on huge quantities of Egyptian corn shipped in from the fertile Nile delta, and on wine and olive oil imported from around the Mediterranean. Some of this economic and organisational activity was under state supervision – the army provided the engineering expertise that built the great aqueducts, for example – but private enterprise did most of the heavy lifting. Food production, maritime and land transportation, storage and warehousing, industrial bakeries, and distribution within cities must have employed hundreds of thousands all told, both freemen and slaves, while ownership was concentrated in the hands of relatively few.

On the other hand, these commercial opportunities were not always confined to the traditional ruling class. Petronius Arbiter in his *Banquet of Trimalchio*, written during the reign of Nero, satirises a *nouveau riche* former slave who has made his fortune in shipping and as a wine merchant: the *Banquet* may be a work of fiction, but ex-slaves, or freedmen as they were called, who went on to make large fortunes were a frequent target for writers and historians alike.

Roman law, as well as Roman society, recognised the importance of the family and provided for the preservation of wealth. In the households of families of standing, a *dispensator* or steward oversaw the management of affairs, while on the family's farm holdings the *vilicus*, or bailiff, performed the role of estate manager. Both posts were occupied by trusted non-family members, quite possibly freedmen or highly valued slaves. Perhaps most significantly, the law provided for the function of *fideicommissum*, a type of legal instrument by which a gift, normally of property, would be held in trust for a beneficiary [such as a minor or an unborn descendant], who could not receive it directly. It was a versatile device which could bypass otherwise tricky legal obstacles. Thus, an unmarried daughter might not be able to inherit directly, but by holding a *fideicommissum* a trusted family friend could ensure that wealth was preserved within the family as the deceased parent intended. The ultimate guarantee was the possession of Roman citizenship, obtained through birth or grant, which protected the legal rights of those lucky enough to possess it.

In short, under Rome the concept of *stewardship* originated, developed, and was enshrined in law. It has proved a vital dimension to the conservation of wealth down the family line.

After Rome

In the centuries that followed the decline and eventual collapse of the Roman Empire, non-ecclesiastical historians of the West largely concerned themselves with the lives and deeds of the ruling classes. Wealth was determined by power, and power was determined by succession, conquest and dynastic alliances. The economic source of wealth remained primarily land. Thus, when William of Normandy obtained the English throne one of his early acts was to establish the national wealth by documenting it in minute detail. The Domesday Book records and values the productive capacity of his new realm down to the last hide and pair of oxen. Under the emergent feudal system, great swathes of the country were transferred to William's followers, and what was not held by the Anglo-Norman aristocracy was owned pre-eminently by the church, whose bishops and archbishops were drawn from the same class. In Britain, at any rate, the oldest family-held economic concerns are in the hands of those estate owners who can trace their lineage back to the Norman invasion.

Prior to the Industrial Revolution, family businesses – trading entities as we would now understand the term – were concentrated in traditional occupations, and locally based. Family Business UK reports that Britain's oldest continually trading family business is RJ Balson & Son, a high street butcher in the market town of Bridport, Dorset. It was founded by one Robert Balson in 1515. However, it is a mere newcomer compared with Japan's oldest documented family firm, construction company Kabushaiki Gaisha Kongö Gumi, which claims a foundation date of 578 AD. Also in Japan is the hot-springs hotel Hoshi Ryokan, which has remained in continuous family ownership through 46 generations, passing through the male line of succession.

Twelve Generations of British Family Banking

C Hoare & Co is the UK's longest-surviving bank and reportedly the fourth oldest in the world. It is owned by the twelfth generation of the family, in direct descent from Sir Richard Hoare, a goldsmith who founded the bank in 1672. It has survived political turmoil, two World Wars, and poor management, which almost caused its collapse in the 19th century. Although headed up today by a non-family member, the current generation of the Hoare family plays an active part in the bank's management.

The bank is famously discreet. Hoare's, as it is commonly known, does not advertise. Customers are recruited solely by word of mouth.

Source: www.hoaresbank.co.uk/our-history; *Through the Years: Tales from the Hoare's Bank Archive*.

Sharp increases in wealth tend to arise when societies are transformed through technological advances, social upheaval, and big political events. The Silk Road – or, more accurately, Silk Routes – stretching across Asia and Europe more or less monopolised intercontinental trade until the mid-15th century. From then on, the dominance of the overland route was eclipsed by the steady rise of the Ottoman Empire, which clashed with the European powers, acquiring a chokehold on trade. The latter turned to the sea and to the bigger, faster vessels which advances in shipbuilding technology made possible. The Age of Discovery had begun. Full-scale replicas of the Golden Hind might look tiny in our eyes, but the ship was robust enough to convey Sir Francis Drake around the world in a single expedition. The English crown licensed piracy in the form of "privateering" and upwardly mobile families like Drake's were substantially enriched by it. Maritime commerce, trading outposts, conquest, and eventual colonisation made the fortunes of families across Europe, as a walk today through the historic quarters of, say, Amsterdam, Lisbon, Venice, or Seville can attest.

The Role of the Founder

At the root of every family dynasty is a founder. That person identifies opportunity in whatever form it presents itself and takes advantage of it: such people conform to the widely accepted definition of an entrepreneur. In the periods prior to the Industrial Revolution, those opportunities tended more to take the form of either social or commercial rather than technological advancement. Frequently, one went hand in hand with the other. The progress of Thomas Cromwell is a case in point. Born the son of a fuller[4] and tavern owner, probably at the very end of the reign of Henry VII, Cromwell rose to become Henry VIII's Chief Minister. The opportunity that presented itself to Cromwell was Henry's break with the Church of Rome and his relentless endeavour to produce a male heir. Cromwell's rise gave him wealth and power, but it was ultimately the whim of the monarch that truncated both his career and his person. There was no dynastic succession.[5] His fate can be contrasted with that of the Cecils, also upwardly mobile in Tudor times, who found favour not only under Henry VIII but also with his father, Henry VII, and the latter's granddaughter, Elizabeth I. The family's possessions still include two magnificent estates, Burghley at Stamford and Hatfield House to the north of London, the titles of Lords Exeter and Salisbury, and the Cecils have produced numerous politicians, two prime ministers and an Olympic gold medallist.

Opportunity in the broadest, most expansive sense arises with the coming of the Industrial Revolution and the seismic changes that result. Canals begin the transformation of transportation, to be superseded by the railways. Steam powers shipping, and shipping the demand for coal, iron, and, eventually, steel. Mechanisation multiplies human productivity, and the growth of mass manufacture creates the possibility of amassing wealth on a scale previously unthinkable for those who are not born into it. The spread of literacy creates vast new markets for newspapers, books, and magazines. What starts in Britain spreads to the United States, a nation always receptive to innovation [and where consumer demand is continually fuelled by new waves of migration from the Old World] and, with something of a time-lag, to the European mainland. Over the same period, the Imperial expansion of the old European powers – specifically Great Britain, the Netherlands, Spain, France, and Portugal – creates new, captive sources of raw materials and in turn new markets to sell to.

The Great Jewish Business Family Dynasties

Out of this maelstrom of social and economic change, in the 19th century there emerges a handful of Jewish families whose names still resonate today: Rothschild, Goldsmith, Sassoon, to name but three. Others, such as the Pereires already mentioned in the Preface, and the Ephrussis, were forces to be reckoned with in Europe in their day. Still others, like the Safras and the Louis-Dreyfus clan, had their roots in the Old World but rose to prominence largely through their activities in the New World. The House of Lazard Frères reversed the process, taking their banking activities from New York to Paris and eventually to London. And there are yet others, such as the Dutch Van den Bergh family, whose business bearing their name was absorbed through merger into the concern that is today, Unilever.

We have discussed above the wider environmental factors that facilitated the rise of these families. To these should be added the changing attitudes towards the Jewish populations in Western Europe, particularly; social prejudice and discrimination remained, but the restrictions on Jewish participation in all aspects of society were progressively lifted as nations liberalised and the rigid ties of the [Christian] church and state were loosened.

Why specifically these Jewish families, and why was their impact so much greater than their mere numbers might warrant? One obvious factor is that following the destruction of Jerusalem in 70 AD by Rome and the subsequent events this set in motion, Jews had for centuries been migrants,[6] existing at the margins of their host societies. They settled across the Mediterranean, in Northern Europe, in North Africa, and as far as South and Central Asia.[7] In many urban centres, they lived in specific quarters, which we know as ghettos,[8] under terms dictated by the city authorities. Many would earn their living by supplying goods and services within their communities; others through trading with or lending money to their hosts. Laws governed their rights and specific obligations to the state, and restricted their choice of profession. In general, they were tolerated if they were useful rather than welcomed, and could be expelled at the whim of the rulers. If you were Jewish, you learned to survive on your wits and to be quick on your feet; it is no surprise that there is a long-standing tradition of great Jewish violinists. Theirs is one of the most portable of instruments, to be packed in its case at a moment's notice.

The best-known of the great Jewish dynasties is the House of Rothschild. Their story illustrates *par excellence* what it takes to survive and thrive as a family business in spite of every conceivable setback. The family has weathered internal disagreements, succession crises, appropriation by government, exile, the tragedies of mental illness and suicide – and yet its members across the various family branches have played outstanding roles in finance, government, scientific disciplines, philanthropy, garden and landscape design, as vineyard proprietors and as patrons of the arts.

Emanating from Frankfurt am Main, the Rothschilds were originally the court factors, or moneylenders, to the regional princely house. The family member who transformed the business from local to multinational was Mayer Amschel, known by his second name, born in 1744. Amschel's stroke of genius was to unshackle his business interests from the court and set up his five sons in the principal commercial centres of Europe at the time: London, Paris, Vienna, and Naples, with one remaining in Frankfurt. It has been said that there are as many mysteries surrounding the Rothschilds as verifiable facts, but there are some things that can be known for certain, largely thanks to the extensive family archives to which historians have had access. The American historian Richard Davis[9] has shed much light on the family's early history through his analysis of the records maintained by the English branch.

Amschel may have been the patriarch, but the driving force behind the business was his son Nathan, who arrived in England, initially in Manchester, in 1799.

His early days were spent not as a financier but as an exporter to Germany of English cloth, for which there was evidently demand. Supported by letters of credit from the Frankfurt house, Nathan made money out of astute buying, manufacturing to order, and by cutting out middlemen. It was only ten years later that he is to be found finally established in London as a financier. Nathan was unquestionably helped by an advantageous marriage to Hannah Barent-Cohen, daughter of a prominent Jewish financier, which launched Nathan into a circle of prominent Jewish families. He also seems to have been greatly aided by rendering services to another German aristocrat, the Elector [Ruler] of Hesse-Cassel, William IX, who was exceedingly rich. Nathan assisted the Elector in protecting his money from Napoleon and was rewarded accordingly. The era of the Napoleonic Wars proved a great opportunity to make money both for Nathan and other members of the family. By 1815, when the Wars were concluded, the Rothschilds' collective capital was put at £136,000 and Nathan's share at £90,000.[10]

From Davis's analysis of the archive, it becomes clear that Nathan was the dominant figure among the siblings. They might not have always agreed with him – in fact disagreements were frequent and often quite vigorous – but in the end, Nathan had his way. His brothers seem to have recognised in him the qualities of a truly remarkable individual: he was commercially astute, widely respected, gifted with an uncanny ability to predict the way things would turn out, and possessed a ferocious appetite for work. He had the attributes of a great leader. The fortunes of the continental Rothschild houses might rise and fall, but the London house remained pre-eminent.

Thus, the foundations were laid for a notable succession. Within two generations, the English Rothschilds were entrenched firmly within the British establishment, ennobled and intimates of high society and royalty. In 1847, Lionel, Nathan's eldest son, was elected to the House of Commons and another son, Anthony, was made a baronet. The offspring contracted marriages between cousins[11] and with the other prominent Jewish families, such as the Davidsons and the Cohens. Family members built a series of great country houses in the Chiltern Hills and the Vale of Aylesbury, to the north-west of London. The bank was established at the City premises from which it still operates, New Court, St Swithin's Lane. Children were numerous and not all were set on a career solely in high finance. One branch distinguished itself in the field of entomology as leading authorities on moths and butterflies. Nathan's grandson, Victor, the third Baron Rothschild, led a remarkable career as variously a zoologist, intelligence officer, and oil executive before joining the family bank as Chairman. The current generation numbers in its ranks artists, writers, film producers, wine-makers, creators of gardens, philanthropists, patrons of the arts

... and bankers. Occasionally, a single member combines a variety of these roles. Today's London house provides the traditional merchant banking advisory services to national governments and corporations, asset and investment management services, and wealth management for families and individuals. It is the last great independently owned and family-controlled survivor among the City's historic merchant banks.

The Rothschild story provides a template for what it takes to create and sustain a great family business:

- A visionary founder [Amschel] with the foresight required to identify opportunities
- The drive, energy, and commercial acumen [Nathan] needed to drive the business forward
- Fecundity – a plentiful supply of descendants to choose from as future leaders of the business
- A willingness at the same time to integrate non-family members into the business at a senior level, to grow the pool of talent and power the firm's expansion
- The ability to structure organisational and personal relationships to adapt to the times and exploit new opportunities
- The capacity to manage disagreement and disputes without destroying the core business[12]
- Resilience, as the family has survived the confiscation of its assets through the Second World War [under the Nazi occupation of France] and nationalisation in the 1980s [again, in France]
- And an ethos that has allowed family members to combine involvement with the bank with fulfilling their talents and ambitions in other fields, or to pursue outside careers

At the same time luck has played a part. This long-lived success has benefited from factors outside the control of more recent generations, most crucially the internationalisation and eventual globalisation of financial services that has gone hand in hand with the upsurge in global wealth.

The Jewish diaspora is far from the only one to provide outstanding examples of family businesses that have thrived in expatriate communities. The Parsis of the Indian subcontinent, originally from ancient Persia, are small in number but hugely influential in business and public life internationally. The overseas Chinese, over 40 million of whom reside outside mainland China, Taiwan, Macau, and Hong Kong, are also a prominent case. In North America alone, it has been estimated that ethnic Chinese control over US$2 trillion of liquid assets [cash or other assets that can be easily turned into cash]. The mainland Chinese economy has undoubtedly benefited from the remittances sent back to family members. Banca March of Spain reports,[13] perhaps unsurprisingly, that two-thirds of companies listed on the Shanghai Stock Exchange are family-managed/controlled; it also maintains that these firms outperform their non-family counterparts. Ethnic Chinese are a major commercial force in other parts of South Asia, such as Malaysia and Singapore, while the East African Asians displaced from Uganda in 1972 have created some outstanding family businesses in the UK.

Out of the Ashes a New Phoenix Arises

"The family tradition was that after completing your education you worked in the family business. I finished university and was told there was no job. So I had to create my own!" – Mitesh Patel, speaking in 2023.

Mitesh Patel is the founder, CEO, and 100% shareholder of Fifosys. He is the second-generation descendant of an East African Asian family that was expelled by Idi Amin in 1972. He started his business in the early 2000s, out of necessity. Over the years, he has acquired five companies and disposed of one for a seven-figure sum – and all from a start-up that began by selling IT services door-to-door for a monthly retainer of £50.

Before their expulsion from Uganda, his father and family had built a number of thriving businesses, of which one was a successful film-processing business. Forced to leave at short notice, the family arrived in Britain with little more than the clothes they stood up in. Over the next 25 years, through relentless hard work, the Patels built the UK's second-largest colour-film-processing business, with more than 90 outlets. At one point, Boots even made a multi-million-pound offer for the firm, which the family rejected. Success brought its rewards, and Mitesh received an excellent education.

The dream was shattered, however, when the arrival of digital cameras around the year 2000 made the family firm obsolete almost overnight. The first ten years of his own business proved a long, hard slog. Operating out of unused space owned by the family business in the West End, Mitesh trudged the streets of London selling technical support services to local traders. In 2010, he enrolled on a business education programme that transformed the company and his own fortunes. From the earliest short-term deals of £50 per month, the company now operates with multi-million-pound agreements lasting up to five years. Its core business today is supplying outsourced IT support to smaller businesses, and Fifosys stands successfully on its own feet. Will Mitesh pass it on to a future generation? Only time will tell …

Source: In conversation with the author.

As a closing observation, it is a tribute to London's openness to international trade that several of the merchant banks that dominated the City during the 20th century were founded by immigrants and controlled by their families: Barings [German], Hambros [Danish], Warburgs [German], to take three. All have since been subsumed by huge multinationals. Today's "banking giant" Barclays has its early origins in the mergers between Quaker family businesses, the Gurneys of Norfolk and the Backhouses of Darlington in the north-east of England.

* * *

The Family Business and the Business Family

The 18th and 19th centuries also promoted a powerful new class of merchants and industrialists who exploited these same opportunities created by a rapidly changing social environment and the rise of colonialism. The British Empire, it could reasonably be argued, ran to a fair degree on beer: India Pale Ale [IPA] was a lighter type of ale first brewed in the 1780s for export to India, marketed as ideal for the subcontinental climate. It was hugely popular with soldiers and administrators employed by the East India Company. The rise of brewing families and their elevation into the nobility created a new coinage, the *beerage*, not always meant as a compliment. For centuries, the British, like other nations, had relied on hydration by ale in the absence of clean drinking water, particularly in towns and cities. Brewing was essentially a small-scale, local affair and often a family trade. New technology transformed the scale of operation. In 1750, a young Samuel Whitbread created the first mass-production brewing operation in Chiswell Street, on the fringes of the City of London and 34 years later installed on the premises the first steam engine, designed by the famous engineer James Watt. The site rapidly became the world's largest brewery. In 1868, Samuel's descendants took advantage of new bottling methods to create a national brand. By 1905, Whitbread's breweries were producing almost 700,000 barrels of beer annually. Between its foundation and the present day, the company has, among other things:

- relocated its headquarters and centre of operations from London to Bedfordshire
- purchased numerous regional breweries
- acquired and then sold spirits brands
- divested its brewing activities and much of its pub estate
- diversified into restaurants and hotels
- sold its Costa Coffee chain to Coca-Cola

Whitbread ceased to be family-owned and controlled when it listed as a public company in 1948. The last member of the family to play a prominent role in the business was another [this time Sir] Samuel Whitbread, who served as Chairman between 1984 and 1992, stepping down from the board in 2001. The current generation is now principally concerned with managing their farming and related interests from the 18th century splendour of Southill Park near Biggleswade.

Meanwhile, a second well-known Bedfordshire-based family of brewing heritage, the Wells family, continues into its fifth generation of ownership of Wells & Co [formerly Charles Wells Ltd]. Following a series of mergers, acquisitions, and disposals, they remain firmly committed to the hospitality industry and to their estate of pubs across eastern England and the northern home counties.

Britain's Brewer

Shepherd Neame stewards the country's oldest surviving brewery, with a heritage that can be traced to medieval times. Once owned by monks, it is located in Faversham, Kent, and is now under the fifth-generation management of the Neame family. Their company is the UK's largest independent brewer, producing around 30 million pints annually, exporting to more than 35 countries and controlling an estate of 290 pubs and hotels across London and the south-east of England. Shepherd Neame has won numerous awards, and its best-known brand is Spitfire, a beer created in 1990 to commemorate the 50th anniversary of the Battle of Britain.

Since 2003, Jonathan Neame has been the company's CEO. The business, he explains, has an unusual share structure. "We are a curious hybrid," he explains. "A private limited company, but also listed on the London market through the Aquis Stock Exchange. The family has control, with just over 50%, the remaining shares being held by a mix of institutions and private shareholders. External shareholding is actually not a bad thing, in my view: over the years, it's been a useful release mechanism for providing family shareholders with liquidity if required. At one time, we had two classes of share, which gave family shareholders additional voting rights in exchange for lower dividends. But that arrangement didn't really work for anyone, so we reverted to a simplified structure, and that seems to work fine."

In line with the firm's Articles of Association, three family members sit on the board. The other five directors are from outside, occupying a mix of executive and non-executive positions. The senior non-executive is external to the family, and Jonathan maintains that the company has to adhere to the highest standards of disclosure and transparency. It is non-negotiable that all shareholders are treated in exactly the same way. On the other hand, Shepherd Neame is a proud, long-standing family business, and that also needs to be taken into account.

"Today we have over 100 family shareholders, and as a board we devote considerable time to ensuring that they understand the business, its values and purpose. As you go down through the generations, you can't take it for granted that the rising generation of cousins understands these things simply by virtue of family membership. Only nine members of the family currently work in the company. In 2003, we created a Family Council as a forum for debate and enhancing the knowledge of all family members about the business. It meets twice a year. We also hold regular events, such as an annual cricket match, which engage everyone in the family, spouses and children included."

"If a young family member wishes to enter the firm, we encourage them to apply, but only for an existing post and on the same basis as other candidates. We do, however, have internships that allow the next generation to work on specific projects that will benefit both them and the business."

What is it that has contributed to Shepherd Neame's longevity and success? Jonathan cites a number of factors:

"I think we have a unique culture of positivity and hard work. Everyone who works for us understands the total commitment of the family. We make a point of celebrating our heritage and our provenance. It's important that we are a company with its roots in Kent, which has a very strong identity, and a footprint that stretches across the south-east as far as the A3, into London and across the Thames into Essex. Beer in this country is a product that has a marked regional character, and you see that in other family-owned brewing concerns, like Adnams in

Suffolk and St Austell Brewery in Cornwall. The relationship with our customers is also very much a two-way street. We reinvest constantly in the business, in our brands and in our estate. It's the opposite of a strictly corporate approach."

On a final note, Jonathan finds the attitude of successive governments confusing. "Unlike in Germany, I don't think there's any deep level of understanding here of what most family-owned businesses bring to the economy: the long-term orientation, the commitment to their workforce, the loyalty of customers. Unlike private equity, profit is not our driving motivation. Businesses like ours are a force for stability and continuity, and the hospitality industry in particular is for many young people their first experience of actual work. Encourage us, and we'll grow!"

Source: In conversation with the author.

Compare and Contrast

These two examples, Wells and Whitbread, illustrate the difference between family businesses and business families, both of which are central to this book. The definition of a family business has already been discussed in the Introduction – it's a concern in which the family retains a significant controlling/managerial interest. A *business family*, on the other hand, is commonly defined as taking one of two forms:

- extended [typically multi-generational] families where a significant number of family members work outside the business
- *or* where the original business has been sold, and the family wealth is now managed collectively by, for instance, a family office [a concept we will examine later].[14]

Wells & Co remains very much a family-controlled and managed business. The Whitbreads, on the other hand, no longer control or manage the business bearing their name, and the family wealth is now diversified. As a general rule, what starts as a pure family concern in the first generation tends to elide into a business family over time and as the descendants multiply.

An alternative way to look at this distinction is as a spectrum, rather than as an either/or divide. Thus, "Rothschilds," which is widely seen as a family firm, is really a term for a multi-generational collection of businesses still under [diversified] family control, but where the family members who still work in the business entities at a senior level are greatly outnumbered by non-family members. The current clan sit somewhere in the middle of the line between family business and business family.

Winners and Losers

Throughout history, family fortunes have been amplified or revived through the injection of new blood and favourable alliances. When Henry II of England married Eleanor, Duchess of Aquitaine, in 1154,[15] she brought with her the rich agricultural lands of south-west France, roughly the size of England south of the river Thames, stretching from Bordeaux to the Pyrenees. The English House of Plantagenet retained overlordship of Aquitaine for three centuries before finally ceding control to the armies of the French King at the conclusion of the Hundred Years War. While it lasted, it was a good run and promoted the fortunes of both Bordeaux and Bristol as ports for the export and import of wines and spirits.

Some centuries later, many members of the British aristocracy contracted transatlantic marriages out of necessity, to boost declining fortunes.[16] The great agricultural depression is usually dated between 1873 and 1896, triggered by a series of poor harvests, accompanied by years of severe rainfall which began in the 1870s. In the years before, English wheat producers had enjoyed a golden period of high yields and good prices, but that began to change with the opening up of the American prairies to homesteaders following the end of the Civil War in 1865. American wheat production boomed, and so did its exports, as the price of transportation across the Atlantic steadily reduced. The combined effect of cheap imports and reduced productivity affected English land values, dramatically cutting the wealth of the great landowners and their capacity to borrow against their assets.

America also provided the solution. Eligible heiresses flocked to marry into impoverished aristocratic families. Shortly after their wedding, Consuelo Vanderbilt was reportedly told by her husband, Charles Spencer-Churchill, 9th Duke of Marlborough, that he had married her to save Blenheim Palace. Consuelo was named after her half-Cuban godmother, who in 1877 had herself married George Montagu, Lord Mandeville and future Duke of Manchester, a man also in search of a fortune from the New World. Winston Churchill, a grandson of the 7th Duke of Marlborough, was the son of Jennie Jerome, daughter of Leonard, the one-time "King of Wall Street," and indeed a frequent business party to the dealings of Cornelius Vanderbilt, grandfather of Consuelo. Titles were traded for wealth. The Anglo-American web of high society was tightly woven.

[In a more recent age, the American Kennedy family is related to the Dukes of Devonshire through Kathleen, the sister of President John F Kennedy. She was briefly married to the Marquess of Hartington, heir to the 10th Duke, until he died on active service towards the end of the Second World War. She remarried, to the 8th Earl Fitzwilliam, only to die in a plane crash four years after her first husband's death.]

In the game of social mobility, there tend to be winners and losers, as some of the incumbents at the top are displaced by the new arrivals. The wealth of the new entrants into the higher echelons of British society was founded on commerce, not agriculture [though the arrivistes were quick to establish themselves with grand country houses and estates]. Those aristocratic families who failed to move with the times or simply squandered their inheritances were met with disdain. In a celebrated speech given at Newcastle on 9 October 1909, the future Liberal Prime Minister Lloyd George railed at the parasitism [as he saw it] and profligacy of the traditional ruling class: "A fully-equipped Duke costs just as much to keep as two Dreadnoughts;[17] and Dukes are just as great a terror and they last longer." The Dukes of Manchester referred to above were notoriously spendthrift: the 19th-century marriage to an American heiress brought only a brief respite. In 1950, the English family seat near Huntingdon, Kimbolton Castle, was sold to a private school, and five years later Tandragee Castle, their seat in Northern Ireland,[18] was also disposed of. Further acreage was divested, but money continued to run through the ducal hands. The 11th, 12th, and 13th Dukes have all had criminal records: the current Duke, Alexander, lives in the United States, holds both British and Australian citizenship, and has served multiple jail sentences.[19] At the other extreme, through the Grosvenor Group the present [7th] Duke of Westminster owns, among other things, around half of Mayfair, 300 acres of Belgravia, almost 40,000 acres in Scotland and a large slice of Cheshire. At mid-2024 he was ranked the 14th richest person in the UK.

Contrasting Fates: [Non-Royal] Modern English Ducal Families

Beaufort: family seat at Badminton, Gloucestershire, with 52,000 acres

Bedford: family seat at Woburn Abbey, Bedfordshire, with 3,000 acres, and large parts of Bloomsbury, central London

Devonshire: principal family seat at Chatsworth House, Derbyshire. The estate across Derbyshire and Staffordshire covers 35,000 acres

Grafton: family seat at Euston Hall, Suffolk, with 11,000 acres spanning Norfolk and Suffolk

Manchester: still extant, but no family seat. The current Duke resides in the United States

Marlborough: family seat at Blenheim Palace, Oxfordshire. The estate covers 12,000 acres

Newcastle: extinct in 1988 – no family seat

Norfolk: family seat at Arundel Castle, Sussex, with 9,000 acres

Northumberland: family seat at Alnwick Castle, Northumberland, with just under 100,000 acres, plus Syon House and surrounding park in west London

Portland: extinct in 1990 – no family seat

Richmond, Gordon and Lennox [combined in one person]: family seat at Goodwood House, Sussex. The Goodwood estate covers 11,000 acres

Rutland: family seat at Belvoir Castle, Leicestershire. The estate covers 15,000 acres

St Albans: still extant, but no family seat

Somerset: family seat at Bradley House, Maiden Bradley, Wiltshire, set in 50 acres

Wellington: family seat at Stratfield Saye, Berkshire [now owned by English Heritage]; the family retains an apartment

Westminster: family seat at Eaton Hall, Cheshire, with an estate of 11,000 acres, plus large parts of Belgravia and Mayfair

Note: This is not a comprehensive list of the properties and assets owned by all current titleholders and their heirs.

Source: Heirs and Graces, Doughty, Eleanor, 2025, Cornerstone Books, London, passim, debretts.com/peerage/passim.

Astute marriages in modern times have played no small part in maintaining ducal family fortunes: Duchesses of Bedford [Henrietta Tiarks, racehorse breeder], Devonshire [the late Deborah Mitford, entrepreneur], Northumberland [Jane Richard, businesswoman and garden designer] and Rutland [Emma Watkins, CEO of the Belvoir Estate and podcaster] have proved formidable forces in preserving their spouses' inheritances.

Noblesse Oblige Gives Way to Family Philanthropy

In the modern world – at least in the West – we take a minimal level of social welfare for granted. Should we fall on hard times, suffer from ill-health or the afflictions of advancing age, the state will come to our aid. It was not always so. For most of human history, families have been obliged to look to their own resources, to form mutual alliances that afforded some kind of insurance, or to seek the charitable support of the better-off or the church [such as almshouses for the indigent elderly].

Judaism, Christianity and Islam have always encouraged their adherents to give to charitable causes. Indeed, the three great monotheistic religions consider that there is a moral obligation on the part of the wealthy to provide alms for the benefit of the poor. From the Anglo-Saxon period onwards, the Catholic church has received the donations known as Peter's Pence, first as voluntary contributions and then as levies, to support the church's mission to help the poor and defray its own administrative costs. In line with the doctrine laid out in the New Testament that a rich man could not enter the Kingdom of Heaven, medieval monarchs and the nobility secured their places in the afterlife through substantial religious endowments. Over time this trading of money for the promise of the remission of sins and eternal salvation played a major part in the rise of Protestantism, in reaction to widely perceived graft and corruption.

For centuries, the English monarchs washed the feet of the poor at public ceremonies in emulation of Christ's bathing the feet of his disciples, and distributed gifts of food and clothing. Charles II instituted the practice of Maundy money, the giving of commemorative coins to the elderly, which continues in ceremonial form into the present day. The modern Royal Family and many of its counterparts overseas devote a large part of their time to their own charitable organisation, such as The Duke of Edinburgh's Award and the King's Trust [formerly the Prince's Trust], as well as serving as patrons of many hundreds of other charities. It is what is expected of those who enjoy the privileges of birth.

It is during the reign of Victoria that the first great modern wave of philanthropy takes place, less on the part of the church or the upper classes, but instigated by the newly self-made who knew what it was like to make their way in the world. Their efforts were directed at meeting the basic needs of the swelling numbers of urban poor, chiefly food, clean drinking water and, above all, decent housing. The names of some of the more prominent philanthropists live on in the housing trusts and associations they founded and which survive them: for example, the Guinness Partnership created by Sir Edward Guinness, Octavia Housing after Octavia Hill and, best-known of all, the Peabody Trust or simply Peabody, founded by George Peabody, an American banker resident in London. Sir Edward, subsequently the first Lord Iveagh, was the son of Sir Benjamin Guinness, himself a notable philanthropist. The family's brewing interests made them enormously wealthy, and having retired at the age of 40 Guinness devoted much of his life and almost £1 million towards improving the housing conditions of the London poor. Peabody was born in 1795 into a poor family in Massachusetts, and as a banker was drawn to London as the world's financial centre at the time. He was a founding partner of the firm that was to become the mighty JP Morgan and made himself rich by arranging the financing of the expanding American economy, principally its railroads. Octavia Hill was not herself wealthy but came from a family with a tradition of promoting social reform, and was a formidable campaigner.

This drive to alleviate the worst social aspects of industrialisation and urban poverty was not confined to London. The Cadbury family constructed the model village of Bourneville for the workforce of its Birmingham factory. Joseph Rowntree of York similarly created the village of New Earswick, while William Leverhulme, a founder of what was to become Unilever, had Port Sunlight built for his Merseyside workforce. In Bristol, two families, the Frys and the Wills, manufacturers of chocolate and cigarettes, respectively, contributed 80% of the initial funding required to create the University of Bristol. The source of some of that family wealth has been subject to criticism, particularly regarding the raw materials imported to manufacture tobacco products and confectionery. Cacao beans and tobacco were for decades shipped from Caribbean plantations worked by slaves prior to abolition. On the other hand, neither family owned nor invested in these resources, and members of both supported the abolitionist movement.[20] It is perhaps no coincidence that many of those spearheading British philanthropy were Quakers, such as the Cadburys, the Rowntrees, and the Frys [one of whose members married into the Quaker Gurneys of Norfolk]. The ethos of social reform was enjoined by their religious affiliation. Those who had prospered were obligated to help their less fortunate brethren.

The situation was mirrored in the United States, where philanthropy as a social movement gathered momentum following the end of the Civil War. The same George Peabody referred to above was as active in the US in providing relief for the urban poor as he was in London [the town of South Danvers, Massachusetts, where Peabody was born, actually renamed itself Peabody in 1868 to honour his charitable work].[21] The Scots-born Andrew Carnegie, whose ruthlessness had made him a vast fortune in the steel industry, made a point of giving away 90% of his money to charities, foundations and education: he founded the institution which was to become Carnegie-Mellon University, which merged a few years later with a research institute founded by a scion of the Mellon dynasty, Andrew Mellon. Philanthropy rapidly became and has remained a notably family affair in the United States. The Rockefellers, Mellons – of banking fame – and the Fords were all heavily supporting charitable causes by the early 20th century. In the United States, even more than in the Old World, it became more or less a social expectation that those who have made it, whether through good fortune or hard-nosed dealing, should redeem themselves by good works. In many families, it has become a duty cheerfully continued by their descendants, either on a large scale – as we shall see in Chapter 4 of this book – or in a smaller way. A fine and modest example of good citizenship in action at the local level is the annual beach-cleaning of the local Suffolk coast, marshalled by the Adnams family, fifth-generation brewers based in the seaside town of Southwold.

* * *

Good Works or Reputation Laundering?

In May 2023, the British press reported the decision of the University of Oxford to remove the name of the Sackler family from museum galleries, buildings – including a new university library – and academic positions funded by their donations. The decision resulted from a review instigated by the recently appointed vice-chancellor, Professor Irene Tracey. She was following moves already made by the British Museum and the V&A to dissociate themselves from the Sacklers' generosity. Four years earlier, the Tate and National Portrait Galleries had also said they would no longer accept Sackler money. By 2023, numerous American institutions – museums, charities, and educational foundations – had already reached the same conclusion.

Oxford was late to the party. According to the *Financial Times* on 20 February 2023, since 1991 the two UK-based Sackler charities had already given more than £10 million to the university. For many years, the family had been under severe criticism in the US for its ownership of Purdue Pharma, producers of the drug OxyContin, widely considered to be a major contributor to America's crisis of opioid addiction. Between 2019 and 2021, Purdue was subject to multiple lawsuits and eventually settled outstanding litigation cases for US$4.5 billion, payable over several years [CTV News, 16 March 2021]. The company was dissolved and made bankrupt in 2021. Despite these acts of atonement, the family was subject to continuing criticism: on CNN Politics [3 September 2021], they were described as "the worst drug dealers in history … getting away with billions."

Money, it seems, can't buy everything.

Sources: Financial Times as above, www.ctvnews.ca/world/article/judge-says-hell-approve-opioid-settlement-with-oxycontin-maker-purdue-and-sackler-family/;

edition.cnn.com/2021/09/02/politics/what-matters-s ackler-opioid-purdue-pharma

In Conclusion

The written historical record attests to the dominance of family through ancient, medieval and more modern times. The earliest wealth amassed was based on agriculture and property holdings, aided by class privileges, and subsequently through trade and the proto-industrialisation created by the rise of urban civilisation.

- In the West, this evolution has progressed over many centuries, as society has assumed different forms. In the East and specifically China, we have seen that progression compressed into decades.
- The Roman world has the benefit of being extensively documented. Where families are concerned, we can see an increasing concentration of power and wealth as the Republic gave way to the Empire under the control of family dynasties [though ultimately it was the armies of Rome that decided who ruled the Empire]. The legal system established under Rome is one of its most important legacies to the West, preserving and protecting the rights of family heirs, in particular female descendants. Much of the legal systems in use by modern continental European states derive from Roman law. Roman civilisation also created the conditions for social mobility, as men of ambition from the provinces and outside the traditional ruling class seized new opportunities, building wealth for their households.
- The feudal system reinforced social hierarchies and confirmed the power of a ruling class whose wealth was founded primarily on land-holding and the dynastic alliances that featured so strongly in Roman society. The decline of this system and the rise of the merchant classes created new kinds of social mobility and fresh blood among the aristocracy, the formation of new dynasties owing in part to royal patronage.
- The economic opportunities that underpin the accretion of much family wealth arise out of social and technological changes and the clash of empires, such as the progressive replacement of the transcontinental silk

routes by long-distance shipping. Western Imperial expansion and the Industrial Revolution provided similarly fertile conditions.

- At the root of a family dynasty is usually to be found a visionary entrepreneur. Such people may well arise from marginalised and/or immigrant groups on whom restrictions are placed by their host societies: their choice of professions, for example, or their freedom of association. Such circumstances, coupled with ambition and drive, provide them with a strong incentive to succeed despite social constraints. The Rothschild dynasty serves as a prime example of what it takes both to found and sustain a multi-generational, multinational family business.
- Over time, a family whose wealth is based on a business may well transform itself into a business family, whose fortune no longer primarily depends on a single enterprise – or into a position somewhere between these two states, such as the modern Rothschilds.
- As new entrant families arrive in positions of affluence and prestige, some old incumbents are displaced: social mobility works both ways. This pattern is clearly visible in the disparity between those British aristocratic families who have preserved their wealth, often by canny alliances, and those who have not, whether through circumstance [lack of heirs, for instance], profligacy, or poor decisions.
- The philanthropy which was once the preserve of the aristocracy was progressively replaced or supplemented throughout the 19th century by a class of nouveaux riches and non-conformist families. Much of their efforts were intended to address the urban poverty and hardship that was the by-product of industrialisation and a capitalism that was largely unconstrained.
- The case of the Sacklers, however, shows that charitable giving cannot necessarily erase a family's past and rewrite history.

* * *

In Chapter 2, we examine how that family wealth is distributed across the world, and how the accompanying power and influence has shifted in modern times.

Notes

1 More broadly interpreted, historical knowledge is added to by archaeology in its various forms, which, aided by technology, has advanced by leaps and bounds in recent years.

2 The term is related to the Latin *pater*, father, and thus originally signified descent through the male line.

3 In the sense of pre-Industrial Revolution.

4 A processor of wool for cloth.

5 A century or so later, however, an indirect descendent of Thomas's, one *Oliver* Cromwell, deposed the English monarch of the day. An example of karma?
6 A small, residual Jewish population continued to inhabit what the Romans designated Palestine.
7 The Sassoons, a Jewish dynasty originating in Baghdad, were commonly referred to as "the Rothschilds of the East": at one time their influence and global reach was even greater.
8 A term that originated in 16th century Venice.
9 "The English Rothschilds," Richard Davis, Collins, London, 1983. Davis notes that Nathan was his own best publicist and claims Nathan made about his early success should be treated with a little scepticism.
10 Davis, p. 31. In today's terms, these sums made the Rothschilds multi-millionaires.
11 Intermarriage kept the money within the family, but at a price. Periodic mental instability has dogged the Rothschilds over the years.
12 Most famously in the 1980 spat between cousins Jacob and Evelyn over the use of the Rothschild name in Jacob's Rothschild Investment Trust [now RIT Capital Investment]. Jacob resigned from the bank, but no lasting damage was suffered by either the bank or RIT.
13 24 April 2024. www.bancamarch.es/en/news/chinese-family-businesses-which-represent-67-of-the-shanghai-and-shenzhen-stock-exchanges-are-more-profitable-than-non-family-businesses-says-rep.html
14 I borrow this neat definition from Ian Macdonald of Wright, Johnson, & ~~and~~ Mackenzie LLP, in *Family Businesses and Business Families* 2018, Globe Law and Business Ltd [part of the STEP series of Handbooks for Advisers].
15 A marriage portrayed in the film *The Lion in Winter*.
16 The gradual decline from the mid 19th century of the landed families whose wealth was based on agricultural holdings, and the concomitant rise of new wealth made from the railways, are vividly described in Anthony Trollope's *Doctor Thorne*, the third in the *Chronicles of Barchester* series, published in 1858.
17 The largest class of battleship then in service in the Royal Navy
18 Now the home of Tayto Crisps, Ireland's largest producer of savoury snacks
19 The family history is recounted in *The Fall of the House of Montagu*, by Robert Wainwright, published by Allen & Unwin, 2025
20 University of Bristol, Legacies of Slavery Report, p. 4.
21 The Peabody Hotel, in Memphis Tennessee, the South's "Grand Hotel" was also named after George Peabody for his charitable work in the southern states.

Further Reading

The Global Merchants, Sassoon, Joseph, 2022, Allen Lane, London.

The Golden Road: How Ancient India Transformed the World Dalrymple, William, 2024, Bloomsbury Publishing, London.

Roman Law and the Legal World of the Romans, Riggsby, Andrew, 2010, Cambridge University Press, Cambridge.

The House of Rothschild, Ferguson, Niall, 1999, Penguin Books, London.

Heirs and Graces, Doughty, Eleanor, 2025, Cornerstone Books, London.

The Routledge Companion to Philanthropy, 2016 ed Jung, Tobias et al., p. 205 ff, London.

2
The Global Shift in the 20th and 21st Centuries

Introduction

List, lists, and more lists. The world seems obsessed with lists that document human attributes and achievement: the fastest, the tallest, the oldest, the strongest, and, perhaps more than anything, the richest. *Forbes* first published its annual list of billionaires, ranked by wealth, in 1987. *Bloomberg* updates its Index daily, so you can get an up-to-the-minute picture of who's up and who's down. For the UK, the *Sunday Times* [*ST*] compiles its own yearly register of the UK's 1,000 richest people, many of whom are residents but not necessarily British citizens.

A common feature of many such lists is that they rank the wealth not just of individual X, but of X plus family. I imagine this is because in a large number of cases publicly available information makes it difficult to disentangle and isolate the wealth of any one member. Thus, we know from the *ST* Rich List of 2024 that Gopi Hinduja[1] and family, ranked number 1, have an estimated worth of £37.2 billion, and David and Simon Reuben and family, ranked number 3, have £25 billion. Ranked number 5, Sir James Dyson and family come in at £21 billion. The Hindujas, a third-generation family business, control a vast conglomerate of companies spread across multiple industries, employing some 200,000 people. The Reuben brothers made their fortunes from trading metals and property, and as for Dyson, well, it's no surprise to learn that the basis of the family's wealth stems from household appliances, though today Sir James is also one of England's biggest landowners. At number 10 on the list, the Rausing siblings, Kirsten and Jorn,[2] are third-generation heirs to the fortune of their Swedish grandfather, who invented the Tetra-Pak, and have made their home in Britain.

In the top 10 of the *ST* list are seven family groupings. The purview of the *Bloomberg* Billionaires Index, on the other hand, is global. The top 10 spots

DOI: 10.4324/9781003685487-3

are occupied by individuals, nine Americans.[3] With the exception of Warren Buffett [ranked number 5, with US$154 billion], the rankings are dominated by the tech founders: Elon Musk, at number 1; Jeff Bezos, at number 2; Mark Zuckerberg, at number 3, and so on. Once the world's richest man, Bill Gates has to content himself with the number 5 slot – but then he has given large parts of his fortune away. The sums are so enormous, as well as subject to daily change, there seems little point in actually listing them all: even Jeff Bezos's ex-wife, MacKenzie Scott, is ranked at number 44, with a personal worth of over US$32 billion.

The sole non-American who makes it into the *Bloomberg* list of the top 10 is France's Bernard Arnault, Chairman of luxury goods conglomerate Louis Vuitton Moët Hennessy – LVMH – and he is the second-generation patriarch of a family dynasty. But at numbers 11, 12, and 13, respectively, are three members of the Walton clan, owners of the world's largest supermarket chain, Walmart. And as we go down the *Bloomberg* Index, family business owners and heirs start to appear in greater numbers. On the heels of the Waltons at number 14 is Amancio Ortega, founder of Spanish textiles giant Inditex, which owns fashion retailer Zara. After Arnault, he is Europe's richest individual, and likewise a dynast. At number 17 is Mukesh Ambani, major shareholder of Reliance Holdings, another diversified family business empire, with its origins in India. And at number 18 is Europe's richest woman, Françoise Bettencourt Meyers, heir to the L'Oréal business created by her grandfather, Eugène Schueller.

Another trend is apparent as you work through the *Bloomberg* Index. The nationalities of those listed grow more diverse. United States citizens still feature heavily, but at numbers 23, 25, and 26 are Chinese business founders. At number 28 is Japan's Tadashi Yanai. Between numbers 30 and 50, the percentage of US-national billionaires steadily decreases, and other nationalities rise: not just Europeans, such as the Wertheimer brothers who control Chanel, but Chinese and Indian names start to crowd out the rest. And below number 50, the spectrum of nationalities widens still further, to include Latin America, Russia, and Africa. At number 133, Sir James Dyson is the first person identified as British to enter the Bloomberg Index, with his personal fortune estimated at just under £15 billion.[4]

Such lists do not always agree with each other: the methods of data collection almost certainly vary a little, and the daily fluctuations of stock markets have an inevitable impact. The timing of the release of publicly available information is also critical. But the broad trend implied is the same. At the turn of the century, you might reasonably have expected a list such as Bloomberg's[5] to be almost wholly populated by Americans and Europeans. Today, the world of wealth is changing and shifting in its axis from West to East.

The Big Family Business Beasts

In recent years, the spotlight has also shone on the size and value of the family enterprises from which much of this wealth derives. Since 2017 industry periodical Family Capital, in association with consultants PWC, has published its own list of the world's top 750 family businesses.[6] Two years before, in 2015, the University of St Gallen, Switzerland, in partnership with global consultants EY, first published the Family Business Index [FBI].[7] It is updated every two years. Both surveys are comprehensive and draw from the same pool of public information: the overlap, as you might expect, is very considerable. The St Gallen/EY report has the advantage of a head start, and this enables the tracking of trends over a longer time.

St Gallen's Family Business Index is a meticulous analysis of family wealth in the form of business assets controlled across the world. The report profiles and ranks the 500 largest family businesses by revenues generated, by location, by industry sector, by the presence of family members on board, by diversity [by which the authors mean how many firms have non-family members or women as chief executives], by the number of women on the board, by year of foundation and by their number of employees. Collectively, the 500 firms that feature in the 2023 report generate US$8.02 trillion in revenues and employ 24.5 million people worldwide.

These are big numbers. For comparative purposes, the total value of global GDP [gross domestic product] in 2020 was put at around by US$85 trillion by statista.com. The years differ, and large aggregated numbers are never exact, but it would seem reasonable to conclude that these 500 family firms represent between 8–9% of global economic activity. They are, of course, only the tip of the vast iceberg of family businesses worldwide.

To be featured in the list, the firms, of necessity, have to meet some criteria. The business needs to be in the second generation or more: if still first-generation, then at least two family members need to occupy positions on the board of directors, the advisory board,[8] or in the senior executive team. The family also has to retain substantial ownership, either directly or by virtue of a trust: in the case of a privately held firm – such as Mars – that means at least 50% of the voting rights and where a firm is publicly-listed – such as Cargill – the threshold is a minimum of 32% of the voting rights.

Let's take the top ten firms by revenue, as the FBI ranks them. Number one is retail colossus Walmart, whose revenues are calculated at US$573 billion [by comparison, the UK's largest retailer Tesco has worldwide revenues less than a fifth of Walmart's], which is more than twice that of number 2, Berkshire

Hathaway. A further five of the top 10 enterprises are US-based, respectively, commodities trader Cargill [number 3], Ford [number 5], Koch, Comcast and Dell [numbers 7, 8, and 9]. Two German firms feature in the list: Schwarz [consumer products, at number 4; best known in Britain as owners of Lidl stores] and BMW, at number 6. Tenth is Reliance Industries, 44.3% owned and run by the Ambani family. It has fingers in many industrial pies, primarily energy and petrochemicals, and with revenues of US$94 billion is by some measure India's largest corporation.

Broadening the exercise to the top 20 by revenue, we find:

- seven based in the US, as per the top 10
- three in Germany
- two in South Korea
- and one each in Germany [Robert Bosch], France [LVMH], India [Aditya Birla Group], Luxembourg [Arcelor Mittal], mainland China [Country Garden Holdings], Switzerland [Roche Group], Brazil [JBS], and Denmark [A.P. Møller – Mærsk Group]. The authors of the 2023 FBI report that nearly half of the businesses featured in the top 500 are headquartered in Europe, 30% in North America and the remainder are distributed between Asia-Pacific [16%] and elsewhere. Only a tiny fraction are based in Africa [Egypt, Algeria, and Nigeria], Russia, Turkey, Indonesia, and Japan.

In reality, the country of location often gives little indication of where these family-controlled firms make their money, or the national origins of the family. The Luxembourg base of Arcelor Mittal [ranked number 14 by turnover], for example, is the result of historic cross-border mergers and acquisitions, and has tax advantages. The company is the Grand Duchy's largest private employer and operates its steelmaking businesses across the world, with a workforce in excess of 100,000. It is also the world's second-biggest producer of steel. The founder and current Chairman, Lakshmi Mittal, was born an Indian citizen and has become a British national, at the time of writing, resident in the UK. Second-generation CEO Aditya Mittal was born in Indonesia, educated there and in England and the United States. He has Indian citizenship. Nationality is almost a secondary consideration: the Mittals are a global family in a global economy. Or take Aramco, the world's second-biggest corporation by revenue, and not, strictly speaking, a family business. It does not feature in the FBI list: it is majority-owned, after all, by the government of Saudi Arabia and the country's Public Investment Fund, with its headquarters not in Riyadh but in the financial hub that is Singapore. However, both the government and the Fund are de facto controlled by the ruling family of Saud, and the power behind the throne is Mohamed Bin Salman al Saud, to give him his full name, Crown Prince and Prime Minister. More of that later.

Moving down the FBI list, the top 50 enterprises ranked by revenue tell an interesting geographic story. Fourteen are headquartered in North America [12 in the US, two in Canada], and 19 are in Europe. Five are based in India, four in South Korea, two in mainland China, two in Hong Kong, and one in Japan. That's 14 in Asia-Pacific, or 28% of the top 50 [elsewhere, Mexico, Brazil, and Turkey have one each]. The first UK-based business to feature in the rankings appears at number 97: Wittington Investments Ltd, essentially a holding company for assets controlled by the Anglo-Canadian Weston family,[9] such as Associated British Foods and Fortnum & Mason.

Commenting on the top 500 businesses as a whole, the authors observe that their growth is outstripping that of the global economy, at twice the rate of advanced economies and one and a half times the rate of emerging markets and developing economies.

To sum up, while it may be no secret that the balance of economic power has been steadily tilting from West to East, it is the big family-controlled businesses that are leading the charge. When the FBI was first published in 2015, 61 companies from the Asia-Pacific region made the top 500 by revenue. In 2023, that number has risen to 79. That's a 30% increase in eight years. More to the point, these businesses are not mere tail-end Charlies, lagging behind, towards the bottom of the rankings; as noted above, Asia-Pacific make up just over a quarter of the top 50 by revenue. What's driving this?

Globalisation and Its Components

The headline answer, unquestionably, is globalisation, but to answer the question properly it is worth spending a little time on the key components of globalisation. There are, in no particular order:

- tariff reduction
- internationalisation of supply chains
- mobile capital
- the growth in wealth across the world
- the rise of global brands

The fact that big family-controlled businesses are outperforming other, less dynamic firms – as described above – suggests that they are better at capitalising on the opportunities that globalisation presents.

Tariff Reduction

In 1995, the World Trade Organisation [WTO] came into being, superseding the General Agreement on Tariffs and Trade [GATT]. GATT was created in 1947 as part of the "new world order" that followed the Second World War. The primary aim was to make the flow of goods across borders simpler and cheaper by progressively reducing financial and non-financial barriers to trade. The WTO agreement expanded the scope of GATT to cover services and intellectual property. This process of lowering trade barriers was accelerated through the formation of regional trade blocs: the EU [the roots of which stretch back to 1951]; Mercosur/Mercosul [Latin America] in 1991; NAFTA[10] [North America] in 1994; and CPTTP [11 Pacific Rim countries] in 2018.

If you operate your business within one or more of these trading blocs, you stand to gain as both importer and exporter. Of course, free trade agreements have not eliminated every barrier to trade, such as language and bureaucracy, but they make cross-border commerce significantly easier. Since the WTO's creation in 1995, according to its website[11] world trade by volume and value has grown by annual average rates respectively of 4% and 6%. In value terms alone, that amounts to an increase of over 400% by 2022. When goods and services flow freely, average wealth tends to increase, and the more unevenly wealth is distributed, those who are rich get richer – especially if the rise in the value of what is traded outpaces the rise in volume. We are back to the big effect over time of small numbers.

Internationalisation of Supply Chains

Hand in hand with the liberalisation of cross-border trade goes the internationalisation of supply chains. Let's say you make cars like BMW [number 6 in the FBI rankings], or pharmaceuticals like the Roche Group [number 16]. Your directly owned factories are basically assembly operations, creating the final products that are marketed and sold around the world. The complexity of traditional car manufacturing [that is, vehicles powered by petrol or diesel] is staggering. The average car contains some 30,000 parts.[12] Behind a company like BMW stand three levels, or tiers, of suppliers. Tier 3 businesses supply raw materials such as metal, plastic or glass to Tier 2 companies, who fashion these into components such as nuts and bolts. Tier 2 companies supply these to Tier 1 firms, which create sub-assemblies such as gearboxes or driveshafts. Tier 1 companies provide the assembler, such as BMW, with what are effectively kits of parts to be bolted together on site, to schedule. At any one time, the OEM – original equipment manufacturer, as car brands are known in the industry – is managing numerous components sourced from perhaps dozens of Tier 1 suppliers, who are in turn managing their own inventories bought from Tier 2 suppliers, and so on.

While a modern car plant may prefer to transact with Tier 1 suppliers based close by, a fair proportion of all the materials involved in building a car will cross national borders multiple times before being finally assembled. To what extent a Land Rover built in Solihull or a Mini assembled in Oxford's Cowley plant is actually "British" is an open question.[13] All actors involved in the supply chain are also trying to shorten cycle times and minimise their own stockholdings to reduce their working capital costs. Regional free trade zones like the EU are a large part of what makes it possible, indeed attractive, to internationalise the supply chain.

Pharmaceutical manufacturing shares similarities with the automotive industry. A commonly used medication typically consists of multiple ingredients. In past times, these might have been acquired, quality-checked, collated and processed on site at a big pharmaceutical plant. Today, the industry has moved towards a tiered supply chain structure similar to the automotive sector's, and a large drug producer is closer to an assembly operation combining compounds supplied by what are in effect Tier 1 manufacturers, who buy from others further down the supply line. Globalisation is particularly appealing when the costs of transporting bulk chemicals are a fraction of those of car parts, and all made possible by continuing efforts to reduce tariff and non-tariff barriers to trade.

And let us not forget that, given the dominance of family businesses across industries and economies, many of those lower-tier suppliers in both the auto and pharma sectors will be family-owned and controlled, significant firms in their own right.

Such internationalisation is a great arrangement, providing goods flow freely, and the advantages are evenly distributed. Poorer economies industrialise, and richer ones benefit from lower costs. Agile companies find it easier to grow by taking advantage of international opportunities. However, extended and complex supply chains are inherently fragile. COVID-19 raised some serious questions over whether indefinite globalisation is always a positive thing.

Mobile Capital

The question "how much money is there in the world?" might seem fairly straightforward. In fact, it's not that simple. The Q&A website Quora,[14] a well-regarded authoritative source of information, supplies a range of definitions, from US$95 trillion to US$125 trillion to over US$400 trillion. It depends on whether you count money as cash and bank deposits – the lowest estimate; or add savings and money market funds – the middle estimate; or also add all assets that people own [static or frozen money, if you like] – the highest estimate. In the modern world, banks add to the money in circulation by creating credit through issuing loans, and when loans are repaid, the money, or credit, in the economy reduces. Taking this into account, the amount of money is constantly fluctuating. In a world where actual cash matters increasingly less, it is hard to figure out what is "real" money and what is "notional" money represented by credit and debit balances in bank accounts or blockchain ledgers [examined later in this book]. And never mind cryptocurrencies. Beyond a certain point, "money" becomes a matter of arcane debate between economists and central bankers. The point to grasp, it goes without saying, is that a trillion dollars is a lot of money, and many trillions of dollars is an awful lot of money.

The second point to take on board is that money in the 21st century is like water. It is in constant flow. Just as the lowest point draws water, so financial centres exert their own gravitational pull. If you are in a position to invest money anywhere in the world, you have a myriad opportunities and almost as many people to help you do it – in New York, London, Singapore, Hong Kong, Zurich and all the other cities where finance likes to congregate. [The same holds true of raising money.] Billions of pounds, dollars, euros, yen, yuan are traded daily. If an international bank does not have a branch in the jurisdiction where a family wishes to invest their money for business or personal purposes, it will have a local partner. Many wealthy families will choose to manage the potential risks to their commercial and personal wealth by diversifying the jurisdictions where their assets are held. If Europe is in recession, for instance, Asian and US markets may offer better opportunities. Out of the FBI top 50 [by revenue] family businesses discussed earlier, 13 are still in purely private hands. The other 37 are publicly quoted, though still family controlled, meaning that at some point the family has turned a proportion of their wealth on paper into cash.

As a result, it has probably never been easier to sustain and enhance personal wealth. So it comes as little surprise to find a concentration of UHNWIs [ultra-high net worth individuals] located in those centres from which their wealth is likely to be managed. Henley & Partners, a firm that provides location advisory services to the international rich, sets the bar for "super-wealthy" at a minimum of US$100 million: the centi-millionaires. As the firm's *Centi-millionaires Report* states in its Overview:

> These affluent individuals are typically the founders of large multi-national companies *or the heirs to vast family fortunes* [my italics]. There are only

> 28,420 centi-millionaires in the world (as at June 2023), making this a very elite club.

By the time this book is published, there will doubtless be more.

According to the same report, their top ten places of residence are New York City [775], the Bay Area (Greater San Francisco) [672], Los Angeles [504], London [388], Beijing [365], Shanghai [332], Singapore [330], Chicago [286], and the greater Paris area [280]. By this yardstick, 15% of the world's wealthiest cluster in just ten locations,[15] though these places of residence are almost certainly just their *principal* places of residence. Many will keep homes in other centres – New York–London is a popular pairing – and then there are the ski chalets, the seaside villas, the hobby vineyards, the yachts that can be moored anywhere. Some locations also give a clue as to how the money has been made. The Bay Area, for instance, is home to Silicon Valley and the venture capital firms that feed off the technology sector. A fair proportion of this Californian wealth will therefore be self-made as opposed to inherited. The same may well hold true of those based in the relatively newly rich Beijing, Shanghai or Hong Kong, although there is a much higher likelihood that this money derives from fairly recent businesses that consider themselves *family* enterprises. Remember Dr Wu at the start of Chapter 1. American high-tech founders, by contrast, tend to be explicit that they are creating corporations, not family-controlled entities that will pass through to future generations, though the wealth may do. London and the UK in general has a strong reputation for education, and that acts as a pull factor for families that can base themselves anywhere, so this may indicate the presence of more inter-generational wealth. All of these locations are forecast to grow the number of centi-millionaires in the foreseeable future.[16]
It has also probably not escaped your notice that four of these top ten locations are in the US, three in China/Hong Kong, one in SE Asia, and two in Europe. And as the list continues down through the *next* ten most popular locations, Mumbai and Dubai pop up, at numbers 15 and 16, respectively. Moscow is at number 17. Geneva and Zurich also make the top 20, and Monaco squeezes in at number 22.[17] The listing gives no indication of nationality, but with personal wealth at this level you and your dependants are basically global citizens.[18]

And the bar continues to be raised. As the *Financial Times* of 14 October 2024 pointed out:

> Talk to 10 different wealthy industry professionals about when you become super-rich … and you will get 10 different answers.

As the article argues, only a few years ago investible assets of at least US$30 million might, by general consensus, have been enough to make the cut.

By 2022, according to consultants CapGemini,[19] there were some 210,000 of those who cross that threshold. Growing wealth, inflation, and the rise in asset values have combined to the point where private members' club R360 – membership by invitation only – limits admission to those whose wealth exceeds US$100 million.

Global Brands

Accompanying all the above trends is the rise of the global brand. The whole point of creating a brand and protecting it with intellectual property rights is to build something distinctive in its marketplace that has value in its own right. When the topic comes up, most people tend to think of brands they encounter in their everyday lives. Take chocolate, for example. Until 1990, British and continental European consumers had been accustomed to eating Marathon bars. From then on, they had to get used to eating the same thing called Snickers. Parent company Mars Inc., America's fourth largest, privately owned and family-controlled corporation, changed the name to standardise the brand across its markets. The company calculated that the costs of promoting the change were greatly outweighed by the savings in packaging, harmonised marketing, and simplifying the product portfolio. And US visitors to Europe could be reassured that a chocolate bar familiar to them was available to buy on their travels. [The Mars bar, on the other hand, remains a uniquely British institution, formulated to appeal to the nation's sweet tooth.] The change has clearly been a success for Mars, as any customer resistance has melted faster than its chocolate, and the brand performs strongly.[20]

This is merely one example. A vast number of consumer food and drink brands – Coca-Cola, Pepsi, McDonald's, Ben & Jerry's, Pizza Hut, and KFC are just a few that spring to mind – are worldwide citizens. They happen to be American in origin, mainly because the US is a huge market where you can build a significant business before having to trade outside its borders, and also because of the dominance of the United States in the world economy since the Second World War.

The development of the global brand has tended to be spearheaded by giant businesses that have long passed out of family or founder control, but it has created a trend that family firms can take advantage of. Clothing has followed the same pattern as food and drink. Timberland boots, Niké trainers, Superdry leisurewear, Ralph Lauren Polo, and a multitude of other international brands are available in shopping malls and centres everywhere. Their logos convey a certain cachet and command a price premium. In particular, family-founded and controlled businesses have pioneered luxury fashion and its associated accessories, and continue to dominate it. The world's largest luxury goods company, LVMH [in full, Louis Vuitton Moët Hennessy], is a collection of brands that has been assembled over the last 40-or-so years by French businessman mentioned earlier, Bernard Arnault.

The Arnault Story

The original family business created by his father was a construction firm, but Arnault saw a far bigger opportunity in luxury goods. Today's business is by some measure France's largest company, and in 2023 it became the first European corporation to be valued at over US$500 billion.[21] The company controls 75 *maisons* or houses, spanning among other things jewellery, watches, leather goods, fashion, fragrances, luggage, hotels, cruise lines, vineyards, fine wines, and spirits and champagne. Some names you may know include the afore-mentioned Louis Vuitton [luggage], Christian Dior [fashion and fragrances], Hennessy [cognac], Belmond [hotels, trains and cruises]. All are billion-dollar-plus businesses in their own right. In essence, if you have sufficient wealth, you could spend a significant part of it merely satisfying all your luxury needs through purchasing LVMH's goods and services.[22]

Arnault has built his empire through a series of adroitly executed – some might say ruthless – deals. In 1984, he acquired the loss-making Boussac-St Frères Group, which had bought the Christian Dior brand following the designer's death, for a token one franc. By selling off the Group's other businesses and stripping out costs, Arnault returned the company to profit and focused on restoring the spotlight on Dior. Within a few years, he then brokered the merger of Louis Vuitton and Moët Hennessy, and soon after made himself the single largest shareholder. Thus, Arnault had created the financial firepower of a public company, which enabled the string of acquisitions that followed.

Many, if not all, of the businesses LVMH has acquired are famous luxury brands that had lost their way or failed to capitalise on the opportunities of globalisation. Tiffany's – properly Tiffany & Co – is a good example. Founded by a New York jeweller in 1837, the store became a byword for high-end luxury, most famously in the movie starring Audrey Hepburn, *Breakfast at Tiffany's*, made in 1961. This was pretty much the firm's high-water mark, until it was bought by LVMH. After the 1960s, the brand passed from family control and into the hands of Avon. The strategy changed radically, and the brand was now aimed at the mass market, plastered on anything and everything. Avon had frankly no idea how to manage a luxury marque, and the brand was disposed of. In 2021, LVMH acquired a majority stake and helped Tiffany return to its past glories: its 300 stores are worldwide, and it has reverted to high-end silver, jewellery, porcelain, and leather goods.

Much of LVMH's success results from a deliberate policy of giving each subsidiary considerable freedom to operate, while closely coordinating research and development across the organisation. Thus, the brands maintain their individual personality, while overlaps and potential cannibalisation of sales between themselves are minimised.

LVMH is far from the only luxury goods business to have spotted the opportunities afforded by globalisation. The company also holds 20% of the shares of its rival family-controlled firm, Hermès, but only 13% of the voting rights; the descendants of the firm's founder, Thierry Hermès, control just under 75% of the voting rights through their family investment vehicle, and own collectively 65% of the company. There has been frequent speculation that Arnault would mount a takeover bid, but this has yet to happen. With a turnover of €13.43 billion and a market capitalisation of €229.5 billion, Hermès is less than half the size of LVMH. It has, however, grown faster in recent years, is immensely profitable, and competes across the board in many of the same sectors, serving the same population of wealthy consumers from its 300-plus stores worldwide. Chanel, on the other hand, remains privately held, under the control of the Wertheimer brothers, descendants of Chanel's co-founder, financier Pierre Wertheimer, and, curiously enough, is headquartered in London, not Paris. Alain and Gérard Wertheimer both feature in *Bloomberg*'s most recent list of top 50 billionaires, ranked joint 30th.

Creating the Arnault Dynasty

Although LVMH is a public company listed on the Euronext Stock Exchange, the corporation is effectively controlled through the family's holding company, Agache, in which Bernard Arnault's five children each have an equal stake. Arnault himself is the Chairman and CEO of LVMH [not unusual in French corporate governance], and the children mostly hold executive positions within LVMH. As reported by the *Daily Telegraph* on Saturday, 30 September 2023, these are as follows:

Delphine is CEO of Christian Dior Couture, the second largest business after LV, where she had previously been Deputy CEO.
Antoine heads up Agache
Alexandre is head of products and communication at Tiffany & Co
Frédéric is CEO of Tag Heuer
Jean is director of marketing and development at LV's watches division.

In October 2024, the *Wall Street Journal** reported a new deal signed between LVMH and the bosses of Formula 1 Racing, which will give prominence to some of LVMH's star brands. Expect to see Louis Vuitton trophy cases, Moët champagne on the podium, and Tag Heuer reclaiming its title of official timekeeper from Rolex.

The Telegraph describes how the children have each been inducted into the business by shadowing a senior LVMH executive, who reports to their father on the child's progress and aptitude.

LVMH recently raised the age limit of its CEO from 75 to 80. Arnault announced he has no intention of retiring, while Delphine is tipped as the likely successor. French daily *Le Monde* has described LVMH as a state within a state. In France alone, its economic impact comprises 1.1% of the country's GDP.

**Wall Street Journal*, 2 October 2024, referenced by LinkedIn

Sources: Newspapers cited: www.lemonde.fr/en/politics/article/2023/08/07/how-bernard-arnault-the-world-s-richest-man-is-expanding-his-empire_6083553_5.html.

The Growth in Wealth Across the World

Arguably, Arnault's major insight has been his grasp early in his business career of how much richer the world was becoming – and was going to become – over the last four decades. There are, it may be recalled, "*only* [my italics] 28,420 centi-millionaires in the world" according to the Henley & Partners report referred to above. That might be a tiny percentage of the world population of 8 billion, give or take, but it still equates to many billions of dollars of consumer purchasing power, given that this figure also includes the 2,350 US$ billionaires identified in the same report.

And let's not forget those who are merely classed as UHNWIs, whose wealth passes the threshold of US$30 million, which of course includes centi-millionaires and billionaires. The New York real estate firm Douglas Elliman teams up annually with London-based agents Knight Frank to produce The Wealth Report,[23] which profiles the rich from the perspective of property investment. The 2024 Wealth Report identifies 253,066 UHNWIs in North America, their numbers up by 7.2% over the year; 155,232 in Europe, where the increase is much less marked, at 1.8%; 18,790 in the Middle East, up by 6.2%; and 165,442 in Asia, a modest rate of change of 2.6%.[24] The percentages cited represent changes between 2022 and 2023. Add these up, and you reach a global total of UHNWIs approaching 600,000. That's a lot of rich people. What's perhaps even more startling is the rate at which The Wealth Report forecasts this segment to grow: by 2028, their numbers in each of the four regions are predicted to increase by at least 20%, bringing the global total to over 760,000. Far and away the biggest increase in numbers forecast, at 38.3%, is in Asia.

We can go a step further down the wealth ladder and consider the spending/investment power of those who are simply "affluent." Capgemini's World Wealth Report of 2023 defines these as individuals with investible assets of between US$250,000 and US$1 million. [They] "hold nearly US$27 trillion in wealth and represent a large population base."[25] This report represents wealth as a broad-based pyramid with the UHNWIs at the top, the next layer defined as "Mid-tier millionaires" [wealth of US$5–30 million], then "Millionaires next door" [wealth between US$1–5 million]; Affluents – as mentioned above – [US$250k–1 million]; Mass Affluents [US$100k–250k] and the mass market with up to US$100k to invest.

Blips in the Trend

The steady march of global wealth has suffered two major setbacks this century: the banking crisis of 2008–2009, and the COVID-19 epidemic that persisted for two years until starting to peter out in early 2023. These are, however, blips in the trend. It is true that the growth rate of many Western economies has slowed in recent years, but that has been offset by that of emerging and developing markets. McKinsey & Co's 2021 report, *The Rise and Rise of the Global Balance Sheet*,[26] reported that the net worth of the world had tripled since 2000. We need to exercise some caution in how we interpret this: the authors themselves point out that much of this wealth is actually in the form of inflated property prices, and is not invested in productive assets like plant and machinery. It also takes into account the valuation of intangibles such as software and other intellectual property.

There are some other caveats to take notice of. Numbers based on past data tend to be more reliable than predictions, and the further out you forecast the less dependable the numbers are: the only prediction you can make with some degree of certainty is that the [exact] numbers will be wrong. It's also the case that large numbers arrived at by adding together lots of small numbers, or even fairly big numbers, can never be more than approximations. The definitions and classifications used by the organisations that comment on global wealth vary and may produce apparent inconsistencies. Knight Frank's Wealth Report argues that the *number* of UHNWIs has risen and will continue to do so, while Capgemini's World Wealth Report maintains that the *wealth* of the UHNWI population declined during the period measured. We need to distinguish between short-term effects, like the rise and fall of stock market valuations, and the longer-term accumulation of wealth as Warren Buffett's snowball continues to gather momentum.

On the other hand, the reports produced by consultancies, real estate firms, business schools, banks and all the others who have a serious interest in this topic – and I have cited only a small sample – all tend to the same conclusion: there is a direction of travel, and it is one-way. The world as a whole is getting richer, and there is a tendency for that wealth to concentrate in the hands of a small proportion, albeit one whose numbers are growing. At the same time, it is unarguable that in large parts of the world most people, not merely the rich, enjoy a quality of life which their grandparents could barely imagine: greater life expectancy, vastly improved healthcare, extensive social welfare provision and so forth. Just consider the choice and variety of cars available to ordinary Western consumers and their levels of quality, comfort and reliability. Once you enjoy a certain level of purchasing power, there is actually very little difference between the basic performance of the vehicles you can choose to buy: they go forwards, backwards and rarely break down. What you purchase comes down largely to image, styling, and brand loyalty.

The Political Dimension

The nexus between wealth, power, and influence is a tight one. In Chapter 1, we looked at how these three were formerly bound up in the institution of monarchy, rule by family dynasties, which has prevailed over most of humanity for the majority of human history. In the western hemisphere, this structure has either disappeared or been modernised in the form of constitutional monarchies, which serve a largely ceremonial function and act as titular heads of state. The institution of constitutional monarchy has changed this nexus, replacing hard power with a softer kind, much closer to influence. Our rulers in the West are elected. Royal family wealth, on the other hand, remains substantial, even if it is at arm's length and to be enjoyed as a form of stewardship, not absolutely.

A Tale of Two Monarchies

The House of Windsor/Mountbatten-Windsor, the ruling constitutional monarchy of the United Kingdom, is the latest incarnation of a line of descent stretching from pre-Norman times through the Normans, Plantagenets, Tudor, Stuarts, Hanoverians, and House of Saxe-Coburg-Gotha [formed when Queen Victoria married Prince Albert], which was renamed Windsor in 1917 [and latterly, in 1960, Mountbatten-Windsor]. There was a brief hiatus in the 17th century with the Commonwealth imposed by Oliver Cromwell, and every once in a while the country has looked overseas to solve a succession crisis. Charles III, the present King, presides as Head of State over 14 countries in addition to the UK, as well as heading the Commonwealth of 56 independent nations. In 2021, *Forbes Magazine* estimated the wealth of the Royal Family at US$28 billion, though most of this is not personally accessible to its members. *The Guardian* in 2023 calculated Charles's personal wealth at £1.8 billion.*

For centuries, the House of Habsburg was Europe's single most powerful family. Between 1282 and 1918, one branch ruled Austria/Austro-Hungary and others, at various times, Spain and the Spanish Empire [large parts of the Americas, Asia, Africa, and Oceania], the southern Netherlands, huge swathes of Central and Eastern Europe, Tuscany, and the city of Milan. Family members also served as Prince-Bishops within principalities of the Holy Roman Empire prior to the unification of Germany. The First World War terminated their rulership of Austria/Austro-Hungary and other European possessions. The last member of the family prominent in public life was the late Otto von Habsburg, who served as a Member of the European Parliament between 1979 and 1999. Through his marriage to Elyssa Edmonstone, Sigismund von Habsburg, current head of the Tuscan branch of the family, who resides in Switzerland, is distantly related to the present Queen [Camilla] of the United Kingdom. The Habsburg family wealth is not a matter of public record.

*Thursday, 20 April 2023

Sources: www.investopedia.com/ahead-of-king-charles-coronation-here-is-the-british-royal-family-s-net-worth-7486580; *p. 1347 [all references cited] Index: Europe, A History, 1996 Davies Norman, Oxford University Press;* www.thepeerage.com/p39619.htm

In Western democracies, ruling political dynasties are today the exception rather than the rule. Over the last century, it is true, the United States[27] has had the Roosevelts,[28] the Kennedys, and Bushes father and son, Canada the Trudeaus father and son, and the United Kingdom the half-brothers Austen and Neville Chamberlain. Winston Churchill's father, Lord Randolph, was a prominent Conservative politician, but Winston's son, also Randolph, was only briefly an MP and was never re-elected. Neither of the two Winston Churchill grandsons who sat in the British Parliament attained the great offices of state. The British House of Lords had been gradually stripped of its hereditary peers, and the current administration has made it clear that it wishes to see the remnant removed completely, along with a reform of the institution. In Western politics, nepotism, where it exists, is quickly pounced on by the media and has given way, by and large, to accusations of cronyism among the elected political class and their appointees.

Elsewhere in the world, the picture looks very different. In the *Financial Times* on 24 August 2024, the Director of the Asia-Pacific Programme at London think-tank Chatham House, Ben Bland, drew attention to the situation in South-East Asia. Six out of ten countries in the region have, until very recently, been ruled by political dynasties: Thailand, the Philippines, Indonesia, Laos, Cambodia, and Brunei. Scandal or controversy seems to have little impact on voters' preferences: until August 2025 the Prime Minister of Thailand was Paetongtarn Shinawatra, whose father Thaksin was removed in a coup in 2006, while her aunt was removed from the same position by the court in 2014. The Philippines' President is currently Ferdinand Marcos Jr, son of disgraced President Ferdinand Marcos Sr, who was forced into exile in 1986: Jr's mother, the prolific shoe-collector Imelda Marcos, was later extradited from Hawaii on corruption charges.

The form of government also seems to make little difference: Thailand and Brunei are monarchies, Laos and Cambodia are one-party states, and the Philippines and Indonesia are multi-party republics. There is a common factor, however, in the form of family wealth or influence. If the name Shinawatra of the Philippines seems familiar, that's because between 2007 and 2008 Thaksin Shinawatra was the owner of Manchester City Football Club, 90% of which he acquired for over £80 million [despite having £830 million of his assets frozen pending a corruption enquiry], and sold on reportedly for more than twice this amount to the Abu Dhabi United Group, controlled by a senior member of the emirate's Royal Family, Sheikh Mansour. As they say, it's nice work if you can get it. Before entering politics, Shinawatra made his money out of the telecommunications business Shin Corporation [now AIS], the largest company in its sector in Thailand. The sale of its shares made him a billionaire, but his public life has been dogged by controversy. Saving a brief visit to his homeland, he lived in voluntary exile for 15 years. Nonetheless, he was Thailand's first elected Prime Minister to serve a full term of office, and was re-elected to serve a second term. The Philippines' Ferdinand "Bong Bong" Marcos Jr is also the beneficiary of the vast amount of money his father made from a domestic telecoms virtual monopoly prior to his banishment, which has helped to finance Jr's long career in politics. Subianto of Indonesia, son-in-law of former President Suharto, made his money by joining forces with his brother, one of Asia's wealthiest men, and their Nusantara Group controls 27 domestic subsidiaries.

Sultan Hassanal Bolkiah of Brunei, on the other hand, is one of the world's few remaining absolute monarchs. Since Brunei's independence from Britain in 1984, the Sultan has been the country's Prime Minister as well as ruler, the 29th Sultan of Brunei. His net worth was put at US$30 billion in an article that appeared in the *India Times* of 2 February 2022. In contrast to Imelda Marcos, the Sultan collects cars rather than shoes, possessing some 500 Rolls-Royces and 300-odd Ferraris. The monarchy's wealth derives from Brunei's vast reserves of oil and gas.

The extreme poverty of Laos and Cambodia means that it is not wealth which has propelled their rulers to the fore, but their dogged careers in the one-party socialist politics that have dominated their countries since the regional conflicts that have followed France's retreat from empire in the 1950s.

Elsewhere in Asia-Pacific, family dynasties have also had a tendency to be prominent in post-imperial domestic politics: thus the Ghandis in India, the Bhuttos of Pakistan, and the Rahmans in Bangladesh. Even the deposed leader of Myanmar [Burma], Aung San Suu Kyi, is the daughter of the man widely regarded as the father of the Myanmar nation, Aung San, who was the driving force behind making the country independent of British rule. And then there is the ruling Kim family of North Korea, who show no sign of loosening their grip on the throat of their nation. Following the post-war decolonisation by the European empires, there is a clear pattern of family dominance in large parts of the region, where wealth and political control are inextricably linked – and accompanying periodic waves of unrest and even military coups in protest against this. The Kims dare not relax their hold on North Korea for fear of the reprisals that would follow. In their case, it is political control which has made the family rich, though exactly how rich is a matter of conjecture. Where dynasties rule elsewhere in Asia, it seems to be wealth derived from their business affairs that has opened the path to a political career and sustained it.

The Arabian Peninsula

It is in the Arabian Peninsula that the ties of politics and family are most tightly entwined. Thanks to its enormous oil and gas reserves and to some adroit political diplomacy, the region has emerged as a pivotal force in the world economy. Saudi Arabia alone produces around 15% of the world's oil and contains an estimated 17% of global petroleum reserves. The peninsula is home to 95 million people and seven countries, plus the southern parts of Iraq and Jordan. Based on rounded-up 2022 data, the richest nations by far are the states of Qatar [GDP per capita[29] of US$88,000], the UAE, the seven emirates or sheikhdoms that comprise the United Arab Emirates [US$53,000], and Kuwait [US$41,000]. Bahrain and Saudi Arabia tie at US$30,000. These figures, though the most recent available, are by now out of date and almost certainly understate current average wealth. They also give an incomplete picture on two counts. First, the average does not represent the distribution of wealth, which is heavily skewed in virtually all cases. Second, dollar figures are useful for comparative purposes – the equivalent figure for the UK in 2022 was US$46,000 – but they don't take account of PPP, or purchasing power parity: basically, what your local currency buys you in your domestic market. Saudi Arabia's 2022 PPP was more than twice its GDP per capita, whereas Britain's was only marginally higher than its GDP per capita. Filling your tank in Riyadh, not surprisingly, costs a fraction of what it costs in London.

The dominance of family in these societies is striking. Kinship has always been highly prized in the Arab world, and alliances through marriage are formed and strengthened in a manner similar to that of the European monarchs of centuries past. Take the UAE, for example, which was created in 1971–1972. It operates essentially as a federation of seven sheikhdoms, with a population of around 10 million out of which only a minority, 11%, are actually Emiratis, as its citizens are known. The seven constituents are Abu Dhabi, Ajman, Dubai, Fujairah, Ras Al Khaimah, Sharjah and Umm Al Quwain. The three largest, in descending order, are Dubai, Abu Dhabi and Fujairah. The capital of the UAE is Doha [Abu Dhabi] and the federation's Presidency and Prime Ministership are held respectively by Sheikh Mohamed bin Zayed Al Nahyan, ruler of Abu Dhabi, and Sheikh Mohammed bin Rashid Al Maktoum, absolute ruler of Dubai. Al Maktoum succeeded his brother both as Prime Minister and Vice-President of the UAE. To keep things neat and tidy, the President of the UAE [Al Nahyan] also appoints the Prime Minister of the UAE [Al Maktoum]. Both the Maktoums and the Nahyans are branches of the House of Al-Falahi, a tribal clan of long-standing significance in the Arabian Peninsula.

Mohammed Al Maktoum's mother was a daughter of the House of Al Nahyan, while his brother Hamdan is the Vice-Regent of Dubai. Mohammed Al Maktoum is reportedly the father of 26 children, and among his wives and ex-wives is the daughter of the late King Hussein of Jordan, Princess Haya, and his own first cousin, Sheikha Hind bint Maktoum Al Maktoum. In 2021, Mohammed Al Maktoum was estimated to control assets worth $US14 billion, although the distinction between what is owned by the monarchy and by the state of Dubai is a fuzzy one. Al Maktoum has undeniably been the driving force behind the economic development of his country and its diversification away from dependence on oil revenues, now less than 1% of Dubai's GDP. His prime focus has been on real estate, including the Dubai Internet and Media Cities, and hotels such as the Burj Al Arab and the Jumeirah Group. As a result, Dubai is best known now as a centre for business and tourism, serviced by the Emirates airline, which Al Maktoum also played a major role in founding. The diversification is also geographic. Dubai Ports International was founded in 1999 to invest in port and container shipping infrastructure outside the emirate, first in Saudi Arabia and then in Djibouti, India, and Romania. Seven years later, now known as DP World, it acquired the UK's P&O, the world's fourth-largest ports operator. This led eventually to the construction of the London Gateway in the Thames Estuary as well as to ownership of P&O Ferries. [In the United States, however, political opposition obliged the company to sell the ports formerly under P&O ownership to a US-based corporation.] DP World is a significant sponsor of golf tournaments, horse racing, and Formula 1 – in February 2023, it announced a partnership agreement with McLaren. DP World is a subsidiary of Dubai World, itself a subsidiary of "Dubai Inc," the term by which the portfolio of assets controlled by the Dubai state is widely known. The Chairman of Dubai World happens to be Ahmed bin Saeed Al Maktoum, uncle of Mohammed.

Not to be outdone by its neighbour, Abu Dhabi houses the Louvre museum, under licence from the Louvre of Paris, and has been steadily building a world-class collection of art and artefacts. Mohamed bin Zayed Al Nahyan [or MBZ, as he is commonly known] has acquired a reputation as an economic and social liberaliser since he came to the throne as the 17th ruler of Abu Dhabi in 2022. Like his counterpart in Dubai, MBZ has served as head of the main organisations which have promoted the modernisation of both his own country and the UAE. In 2024, *Forbes Magazine* put the wealth of the Al Nahyan family at US$305 billion, declaring them the world's richest family[30] – a financial position derived originally from oil, and since diversified into assets held across the world.

Saudi Arabia

In population terms, Saudi Arabia is nearly four times the size of the UAE and covers a vastly greater area. Forty-two per cent of residents are foreign nationals, and the local population is heavily skewed towards the young: over 60% are under 30 years old.

The kingdom came into existence in 1932 and has been ruled ever since by the House of Saud. In the Arabic form, the full name of the kingdom implies that it is a possession of the Saud family, the Al Sauds. The present Head of State is King Salman, who acceded to the throne in 2015. The line of succession historically is lateral rather than lineal [changed to election by an elite council of princes in 2006], and Salman is the 25th son of the country's founder. The real power behind the throne is Salman's seventh son by his third wife: Mohammed bin Salman [MBS], who, from an unpromising start towards the back of the queue, has manoeuvred himself into the pole position of Crown Prince. In a society where polygamy is the norm among the ruling class, the Royal Family is enormous by European standards. According to Wikipedia[31] royal princes number "at least 7000, with most power and influence being wielded by the 200 or so male descendants of Ibn Saud [or King Abdulaziz], the country's founder." If wives and children are added, the entire family numbers must be many times greater.

The extended family controls the legislature, the courts and the military, not to mention the lion's share of the economy: some estimates of the Royal Family's riches measure their net worth at US$1.4 trillion. That's US$1,400 billion, to be explicit. This figure includes the family's interest in Saudi Aramco, the state oil and gas company, and its vast assets in fossil fuel reserves, making *them* the wealthiest family in the world and the wealthiest in recorded history. By this reckoning, the House of Saud is over four times richer than their neighbours, the Al Nahyans in Abu Dhabi. Once again, the lines between what is the family's and what is the state's are hazy in the extreme. This point is underscored in an article that appeared in the *Financial Times* on 9 October 2024, entitled "Just How Rich Are Arab Rulers?" The author commented on the key points emerging from a Global SWF[32] survey of wealth in the Gulf Co-operative Council [GCC: the coordinating body for all countries on the Arabian Peninsula]. Combined, the ruling families in the region control US$6.8 trillion of assets, equivalent to twice the value of Apple, the world's most valuable company at the time of writing. What do these funds actually do? According to the writer, four things:

- they help diversify the region's asset base away from oil and gas dependence
- they project "soft" power through promoting tourism, entertainment and leisure: think of Qatar's hosting of the 2022 football World Cup, and Saudi Arabia's enormous recent investments in golf
- they buy "garish bling" and "stroke the rulers' giant egos"
- they own "pretty much everything in touching distance" – and that includes the national champions across industries

Together, the ruling families and the sovereign wealth funds own the majority of the shares of the nearly 1,000 companies listed on the GCC's public stock markets

The astonishing rise of the economies that occupy most of the Arabian Peninsula, and their consequent high profile, has made them an obvious target for criticism. In the interests of balance, it is also worth pointing out that their citizens, if not all residents, enjoy a standard of living which their forbears could scarcely have dreamt of. In the last quarter-century, these countries' rulers have made significant strides in changing the economic model from that of pure *rentier* capitalism towards encouraging the rise of a professional class of corporate managers, service providers such as lawyers and accountants, and entrepreneurs.[33]

In Conclusion: The Sources of Family Wealth

At this point, we might well pause for breath and take stock. In this attempt so far to understand the depth and breadth of today's world's ultra-rich clans, some key features have emerged:

- there is a *narrow* way, if you like, to regard and measure the wealth possessed by today's ultra-rich families, generated by their business holdings. In most cases, that wealth derives in the first instance from a business created by a founder or sibling founders, and passed through generations. At some point, a proportion of that wealth in the form of assets is typically converted into cash via a listing on a public stock market. That forms an important element in the valuation approach taken by reports such as St Gallen's/EY's Family Business Index.
- there is an alternative, *broader* approach, which takes the view that in some cases – in effect, absolute monarchies – there is no real difference between what is owned directly by the family and what is owned, in name, by various entities of the state. Take the case of another oil-rich country on the Arabian Peninsula, Kuwait. It is ruled by the Al-Sabah family, another hereditary monarchy, whose wealth as of May 2024 was estimated at US$360 billion. In 1953, Kuwait created the world's first sovereign wealth fund to reinvest the surplus revenues arising from exporting oil and gas. [Such funds are not confined to the Middle East: Norway, another major energy exporter, has two, with a combined value of over US$1.7 trillion. The Norwegian Royal Family has no beneficial interest.] Kuwait also now has two sovereign wealth funds, the General Reserve Fund [basically money for a

rainy day] and the Future Generations Fund, which receives 15% of annual oil revenues. The funds are managed by the Kuwait Investment Authority [KIA], an arm of the state. As of late 2023, it had over US$800 billion under management. Among other assets, the KIA owns the London department store Harrods outright, but most of its investments consist of significant minority holdings in large quoted companies such as Amazon. The KIA has a well-defined corporate governance structure, consisting of a board of directors, headed by the country's Finance Minister, and an executive management board of investment professionals.

- two of the six members of the board of directors also happen to be members of the Al-Sabah family. To be clear, the financial affairs of the KIA and those of the Al-Sabah family are formally separated, and the beneficiaries of Kuwait's sovereign wealth funds are the current and future citizens of Kuwait. On the other hand, it seems most unlikely that the KIA would make any decision that runs counter to the interests of the ruling family, and that the latter's position is secure so long as the largesse generated by the sovereign wealth funds – and distributed to the population – continues to flow.
- it is also clear that the source of modern family wealth is closely tied to history, geography, and natural resources. Large parts of the world were under the colonial rule of European powers until the mid-20th century, and some regions for centuries. During that time a significant part of most such nations' wealth was transferred across the world, as raw materials were transformed into higher value finished products: for example, raw cotton from India was turned into clothing in the mills of Lancashire and palm oil from Indonesia, Malaysia, and West Africa was used to produce soap in Port Sunlight, Merseyside, and margarine in Holland. Commodities were exported to industrialised economies and, in many cases, imported by the original producing countries as finished products. Black tea, for instance, in the form most widely consumed by Western tea-drinkers, is largely produced on estates in East Africa and South Asia. Historically, the supply chain has consisted of bulk exports to the West, where it would be blended and packed in factories, transformed from commodity leaf into teabags. A large proportion of the world's biggest-selling black tea brand, Lipton Yellow Label, was for years produced by Unilever in its Leighton Buzzard factory in Bedfordshire and exported back east to markets in the Middle East and north Africa;[34] rival Twinings is still blended and packed in Andover, Hampshire, and according to the company's website is enjoyed by consumers in over 130 countries.

Parent company Associated British Foods is in turn owned by UK-based Wittington Investments, ranked 97 in the St Gallen/EY FBI list, which holds the business interests, you may recall, of the Anglo-Canadian Weston family.

- as noted already, since the dissolution of Western empires and the granting of independence, a relatively small number of families in post-colonial countries have made themselves prominent in politics and wealthy in the extreme. As this transfer of power has occurred very largely within the second half of the 20th century, these new, emerging dynasties are concentrated in the first and second generations.
- there is an interesting parallel with the collapse of the old Soviet Empire. When that fell apart in the late 1980s/early 1990s, a new version of entrepreneurial self-enrichment was unleashed. In the case of Russia, that largely took the form of the asset-stripping of the old state-controlled heavy industries, such as steel and mining. Almost overnight, a new class of "oligarchs" emerged, the source of whose wealth under Putin's administration is often obscure [and obscured]. The widespread enforcement of sanctions and confiscation of bank accounts and other assets since the invasion of Ukraine means it is too early to tell whether this wealth can be sustained through the generations. Other components of the old Soviet bloc took a different direction, towards representative democracy, looked westward, and joined the European Union. None of these countries yet host family businesses which appear in the FBI Index top 500 – it is too soon. On the other hand, an emerging generation of Eastern European entrepreneurs is beginning to make their presence felt. EY's World Entrepreneur of the Year™ 2022 was Poland's "king of lockers" for e-commerce parcel deliveries, Rafał Brzoska, whose business InPost came to the Euronext Amsterdam stock market in 2021. While we are on the subject of Poland, that country's economic performance since liberation from communist control has been astounding: in 1990, its economy was the same size as Ukraine's. By the time just prior to Russia's invasion, it had grown to four times that of its less fortunate neighbour. The Czech Republic's richest man is self-made 49-year-old Daniel Křetínský, whose personal wealth was put at US$9.6 billion by *Forbes Magazine* in 2024. His business interests embrace heavy industry, media, football clubs – he is the largest shareholder in West Ham – and most recently a successful bid for control of the UK's Royal Mail. Where they have led, others follow – perhaps creating the family dynasties of the future.

A Tale of Two Companies

In 1927, two Dutch family-owned businesses, Van den Bergh and Jurgens, merged to form the Margarine Unie, or Margarine Union, the Netherlands' largest producer of edible fats and oils. Other family interests, arising from previous acquisitions, were also involved. Two years later, this Rotterdam-based giant united with the UK's largest soap manufacturer, Lever Brothers, to create what we now know as *Unilever*. As the business expanded through organic growth and acquisition, its ownership diversified, assisted by a unique dual-listing structure on the London and Amsterdam stock exchanges. At the time of writing, it is the world's sixth-largest consumer goods company by sales, owning such global brands as Ben & Jerry's, Magnum, Dove, Persil/Omo, Lipton Ice Tea, Vaseline and Domestos. The founding families ceased to control the business many years ago.

A major attraction of the merger between the Margarine Unie and Lever Brothers will have been the complementary nature of their markets: the Dutch empire embraced the island archipelago of Indonesia, and the British, India and Malaysia. These territories provided huge quantities of the palm oil used to produce soap and edible fats, as well as millions of consumers for finished goods.

The *Louis Dreyfus* company, ranked number 29 in the Family Business Index, was founded by a teenage entrepreneur, Léopold Louis-Dreyfus, in 1851, who traded cereals between France and Switzerland. Today, it has revenues worldwide of around US$50 billion and is one of the big four traders of agricultural commodities. The company is the world's biggest trader of cotton and rice. It is also a major trader of metals, chiefly copper, zinc and lead concentrate. The business is controlled by a parent holding company from the World Trade Centre in Amsterdam and maintains a head office in Rotterdam. Different branches of the family oversee various divisions based in Europe and the United States. Like the Rothschilds, the Louis-Dreyfus family is Jewish and had its European assets confiscated by the Nazis during the Second World War. Unlike Unilever, which is largely owned by financial institutions, the Louis Dreyfus company remains private and is 94% owned by Léopold's descendants. Its best-known member is the actress Julia Louis-Dreyfus.

Source: public data.

- in Western Europe, history has favoured the longevity of multi-generational family businesses. Germany has two companies in the St Gallen FBI top 10, seven in the top 50 and 72 in the top 500. You may well recognise names outside the top 50 such as Axel Springer [publishing], Dr Oetker [food], Aldi [retail: as mentioned, rival Lidl is controlled by the Schwarz family, ranked fourth] and a host of manufacturers such as Jungheinrich, Vaillant and Miele. Some of the 72, towards the bottom of the ranking, are considered part of Germany's Mittelstand, the medium-sized, mainly family-controlled businesses that comprise the backbone of the country's economy. The bias in Germany is more towards industrial manufacturing in "heavy" industries; in Spain, Portugal, and Italy more skewed towards artisan sectors such as textiles and leather goods. But with such a dominant presence in every national economy, family businesses will be found across all sectors, and that is reflected in the make-up of the FBI, including in North America. The notable omission, as already discussed, seems to be the technology sector, dominated by the US, where founders create corporations, not dynasties.

* * *

In Chapter 3, we will see how the wealth amassed by these families is sustained and how their lifestyle is supported by a complex eco-system of service providers.

Notes

1 Whose death was reported just as this manuscript was submitted to the publisher.
2 With sibling Finn, the two Rausings control the Tetra Laval group.
3 Data drawn from the *Bloomberg* Billionaires Index published on 8 April 2025.
4 It is unclear how *Bloomberg* isolates Sir James's personal wealth from that of the rest of the family.
5 Unfortunately it was first compiled in 2012, so a direct comparison is not possible.
6 www.famcap.com/https-www-famcap-com-2023-02-the-worlds-top-750-family-businesses-a-visual-guide/
7 Viewable at https://familybusinessindex.com
8 Individual jurisdictions, such as Germany and Switzerland, require different company governance structures from, say, the US or the UK.
9 The family controls a second holding company based in Canada, George Weston Ltd.

10 Amended but not significantly changed to the USMCA agreement in 2020 under Donald Trump's Presidency
11 www.wto.org/english/res_e/statis_e/trade_evolution_e/evolution_trade_wto_e.htm#:~:text=World%20trade%20values%20today%20have,the%20WTO%20was%20first%20established
12 www.indx.com/en/posts/driving-innovation-for-automotive-suppliers#:~:text=The%20automotive%20supply%20chain%20can,parts%20needed%20by%20Tier%201
13 Both operations are of course owned by foreign companies.
14 www.quora.com
15 A similar pattern holds true of the world's 2,350 US$ billionaires, according to the same report.
16 The present UK government, however, seems to be creating policies that reverse this trend.
17 Although at only 0.78 $miles^2$ Monaco more than pulls its weight.
18 In the *Financial Times* on 6 September 2024, Lisa Freedman outlines some of the pros and cons which influence the international rich in their choice of domicile.
19 World Wealth Report 2023.
20 In September 2024, following the vogue for nostalgia, Mars actually reintroduced the Marathon brand to the UK.
21 As indicated earlier, Arnault [plus family] is the only non-US tech entrepreneur to make into the global top 10 wealth list; in August 2024 Arnault's personal wealth was put at US$180 billion.
22 Following the death of Giorgio Armani in September 2025, LVMH was widely mooted to be front-runner to acquire the Armani empire as well.
23 www.knightfrank.com/wealthreport
24 The continent of Africa is a notable omission, perhaps because many seriously rich Africans maintain a primary residence outside their countries of origin.
25 CG WWR 2023, p. 5.
26 www.mckinsey.com/industries/financial-services/our-insights/the-rise-and-rise-of-the-global-balance-sheet-how-productively-are-we-using-our-wealth
27 In the 21st century Donald Trump may be attempting to create one: see *Bloomberg Morning Briefing, Americas Edition*, 22 May 2025.
28 From the same clan, but different branches.
29 National wealth divided by the population.
30 www.news18.com/business/meet-abu-dhabis-al-nahyan-the-richest-family-in-the-world-8864323.html
31 Based on a *Financial Times* profile of 30 September 2010.
32 https://globalswf.com/, a platform that tracks the value of sovereign wealth funds worldwide.
33 See, for example, Prince Mohammed Bin Salman College of Business & Entrepreneurship – MBSC. www.mbsc.edu.sa
34 The factory was closed in the late 1990s and production moved to the Jebel Ali free zone in Dubai. Shipping costs reduced dramatically as a result.

Further Reading

The Billionaire Raj: A Journey Through India's New Gilded Age, Crabtree, James, 2018, Crown Publishing Group, New York.

MBS: *The Rise to Power of Mohammed Bin Salman*, Hubbard, Ben, 2021, William Collins, London.

3
The Social Network: The System That Preserves and Grows Family Wealth

In Chapters 1 and 2, we discussed the history and emergence of family businesses as a dominant force in the world economy. Regardless of whether that wealth is generated very largely by a business which the family still controls, or by business interests funded by the sale – whole or in part – of the original business, the scale of wealth possessed by the families at the top of the pyramid is breathtaking.

The Property Finder

Domus Holmes is a fully independent, Bristol-based, property search and buying agency founded in 2015 by Jerome Lartaud and his wife, Claire Russell-Lartaud, a property solicitor.

Domus Holmes provides a comprehensive and bespoke property search and acquisition service, operating predominantly in the south-west of England in cities such as Bristol, Bath, and the surrounding counties, but also with an international outreach. The company focuses on prime and super-prime properties. At any one time, between 15 and 20 clients are on the books, split more or less 50/50 between UK residents and overseas buyers.

Around half of the clientele are ultra-high-net-worth [UHNW] families with a budget starting at £6 million. They come to Domus Holmes through referral from the company's extensive network of professional contacts: primarily lawyers, private bankers, consultants, and the Private Offices which manage family wealth. "Three-quarters of our clients are seeking a country house in the UK to establish a presence here, or to find a suitable location for their children's education," says Jerome. "The south-west has excellent schools, many in beautiful

DOI: 10.4324/9781003685487-4

settings. A client stays with us until we find the right property for them. The greatest challenge is understanding what they want, which is not always what they think they need. For example, there has been an explosion of interest in the Cotswolds; in the trade, we tend to call it the Clarkson effect. It created a rise in the number of property search agencies as well! We undertake searches in the Cotswolds, of course, but we might also show a client properties in an area they haven't considered, such as Somerset. There are just as many beautiful villages and fine houses, but the buyer gets more for their money, and the roads are less crowded."

"During Covid, we were exceptionally busy. Now things have settled down, and client requirements are changing. In the pandemic, people were desperate for maximum space and isolation. Now they realise the benefits of being close to good transport links to London and airports such as Bristol, not to mention local amenities like a village pub. Some clients are keen to follow trends – when celebrities are featured with outdoor kitchens, for instance, then they must have one as well. Others are more inclined to go their own way. In the next few years, I think more clients will be looking not just for a house, but for agricultural opportunities offered by land. I can see vineyards becoming increasingly sought-after, and a demand for other possibilities that enable an estate to pay for itself. So long as we have great schools and high-end clients, this is a business that will continue to do well. We only ever work for the buyer, and that way we can ensure no conflict of interest."

Source: Conversation with the author.

Given the loyalty of their customers, it is perhaps no surprise that so many upscale brands are family-owned and managed, whether they be the wines and spirits of Berry Bros & Rudd [in its tenth generation of family control and management], the leather goods, fragrances, and apparel of Hermès, the jewellery sold by Boodles [now under the sixth generation], or the luxury maisons of Arnault's vast conglomerate, LVMH. In many cases, the founding family names are still above the door, creating an expectation of personal service and exquisite attention to detail. Admittedly, neither Fortnum nor Mason still runs the eponymous store in Piccadilly, but that perception of quality and service has been painstakingly maintained by the current proprietors, the Weston family. Global PR firm Edelman's 2023 Trust Barometer international survey reported that family-owned firms enjoy a "trust advantage" – trusted, that is, to do what is right – of 9% over non-family private firms, 12% over public companies, and a remarkable 17% over state-owned entities.[1]

It is perhaps more intriguing to discover that many more everyday brands, which you had assumed were still owned by the original founders or had passed into the hands of corporations, are ultimately under family ownership. Like me [before I began the research for this book], in all probability you have never heard of JAB Holdings. The company prefers discretion. JAB Holdings, formerly Joh[annes] A Benckiser Holdings, is based in Luxembourg, and is the investment vehicle controlled by four members of the Reimann family. They are descendants by adoption of Albert Reimann Jr, himself a lineal descendant of the co-founder of the Benckiser chemical company. The family has long parted company from the business, now Reckitt-Benckiser, which bears its name. As of mid-2024, each of the Reimann quartet owns an equal share in this master investment vehicle, which has over US$50 billion of assets under management. The latest valuation in the public domain of each owner's share is almost US$4 billion, and that dates from 2015. It can be safely assumed that the value has since increased significantly. Among JAB's Holdings' investments is a 60% majority shareholding in cosmetics brand Coty, a 27% stake in soft drinks group Keurig Dr Pepper, and outright ownership of Krispy Kreme doughnuts and food takeaway retailer Pret A Manger. In the course of some 40 years, the assets managed by JAB Holdings have risen 500-fold, making the foursome Germany's second richest family after the Kuehne transportation dynasty. They are not the only ones to have benefited. The two partners who manage JAB Holdings on the owners' behalf, Peter Harf and Olivier Goudet, are, according to Bloomberg,[2] themselves billionaires. Harf, Goudet and many others like them are a vital part of the eco-system which preserves and enhances the wealth and well-being of the world's ultra-rich families.

The scope of this chapter is the identification and mapping of those elements that make up that eco-system. We can represent them in the graphic overleaf: In much the same way as a king or emperor would maintain a court or retinue of administrators and advisors, so the modern, seriously wealthy, multi-generational family relies heavily on a circle of professionals. Some may be inherited, passed between the generations, and some may be chosen by the rising generation for a new or specific purpose. They serve different functions, but must meet the common criteria of trust and discretion. They are, after all, privy to the family's secrets and have access in many instances to vast sums of money.

In the graphic below, the network is divided between those professionals whose role is primarily to support the family's business interests – the right

UHNW Family Business or Business Family: Networks of Support

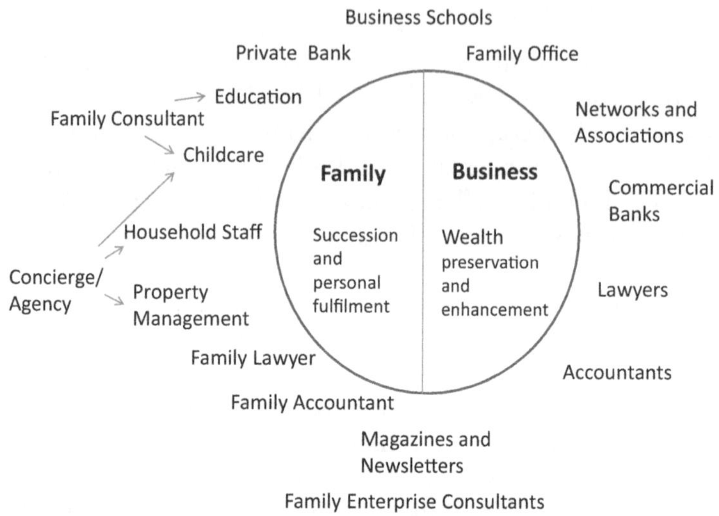

Roles & Responsibilities

Mainly individuals

- Family
- Private Bank: looks after all routine & special personal family member banking needs
- Family Consultant: long term planning for family next generation[s]
- Household Staff: look after properties worldwide
- Childcare : early years specialists
- Education: elite schools and universities
- Property Management: sources family's property requirements
- Concierge/Agencies: often manage staff, childcare, property
- Family Lawyer: understands personal impact of global lifestyle and issues
- Family Accountant: minimises worldwide tax liabilities

Mainly institutions

- Business
- Family Office: manages portfolio of investments
- Commercial Banks: provide funding as required for acquisitions or disposals
- Lawyers: specialists in commercial transactions
- Accountants: specialists in commercial transactions

Business Schools and Support Networks, Publications, and Newsletters

Note: there may be strong overlaps between Business and Family lines of responsibility and one institution may fulfil multiple roles.

Figure 3.1 UHNW family business or business family: Networks of support
Source: The author.

hemisphere; and those whose role is to support the family in a private capacity – the left hemisphere. The organisations that straddle both hemispheres, business schools, magazines and newsletters, support the family in both a personal and business capacity.

It's a theoretical model, simplified to represent an increasingly complex ecosystem. In practice, there is often a degree of crossover between hemispheres. A family might use the same multi-disciplinary firm of accountants or lawyers to advise on both personal and commercial matters, such as taxation, or cross-border residential and trading strategies. Family enterprise consultants also bridge the two hemispheres. I was recently asked by a friend who works in private banking about early years' childcare. A client had raised this topic in conversation and expected him to provide advice. How do you find a good children's nanny, my friend asked me.[3] Other families might choose to keep the boundary between business and family absolutely watertight, for reasons of confidentiality or because that is the family tradition.

A Fictional, but Representative, Case

The requirement for this type of advisory network and the need to expand it tend to increase as the generations multiply. Let's take a fairly typical imaginary example, a wealthy family now in its third generation. The family derives its wealth from a *first-generation* business started by a husband and wife – call them A and B – in their 30s. At start-up, the couple are the sole shareholders and the business becomes highly successful. Over the years, it generates sufficient income to provide the family with a large house in the suburbs, a holiday home in the Caribbean and the ability to educate their three children at elite schools and universities. When the couple in their 70s choose to start transferring ownership to the next generation, they have personal wealth of around £5 million – excluding their shareholding in the business and their own property – invested in a range of assets. That wealth has accrued from three sources:

- the salaries they have paid themselves from the business, which cover their daily living expenses and financial commitments
- the dividends they have taken out of the business over the years and reinvested
- and the rise in the value of the portfolio of assets they have invested in

The income from that personal wealth is sufficient to secure all their needs in retirement and to put money in trust for the education of their grandchildren [five at the time of retirement].

The *second generation*: When their parents retire, the three children – C, D, and E – each receive 20% of the shares. The remaining 40% stay with the founders. A formula has been devised that enables the remaining shares to be vested in the second generation over time, subject to each recipient continuing to work in the company. After completing their higher education, C and D choose to work in the family business. E, on the other hand, has from an early age shown an interest in medicine and decides to train as a doctor. She has no interest in a career in the family business, which, in any case, is not in the life sciences sector. She does, however, retain her 20% shareholding bequeathed by her parents, which entitles her to the same voting rights and receipt of dividends as her two brothers, C and D: she forfeits only her right to receive additional shares from her parents. As a result, that 40% still in first-generation ownership vests over time equally between the two siblings who stay with the firm, until by the time of their parents' death, C and D will each own 40% of the company.

The brothers have different but complementary talents. C is by nature a trader and deal-maker, adept at spotting opportunities and negotiation. D is a builder of businesses. He likes to develop a company's potential and to spend time creating management teams in the subsidiaries which the family firm acquires. In the space of 20 years, the firm has transformed itself from a specialist publisher of regional newspapers to a proprietor of national and international magazines in several niche sectors, the owner of its own advertising and web design agency network, and part-owner of three printing firms outside their home country. The firm now has offices in London, New York, and Singapore, which requires constant travel on the part of the brothers. The consequence is that sibling C and his wife decide to move to the United States full-time and raise their two children in New York, while D, his spouse, and their family of two remain in London. The business remains private, under the sole control of the family and now generates sufficient cash to pay its shareholders substantial annual dividends of millions of pounds. After two decades, the second generation has migrated from being merely wealthy to being rich. C, D, and E are UHNW individuals in their own right.

For E, unfortunately, things have not worked out so well. In her 20s, she moved from the UK to Italy to marry someone she met while at medical school. She and her husband had one child, a boy, before deciding to separate some years later. Now he has met someone else and wants a divorce. E is an Italian citizen, and her estranged husband is seeking a divorce in Italy, under Italian law. Of the two, E is considerably wealthier, and if she wants primary custody rights over their son it looks likely that she will have to make a big financial settlement in her husband's favour. His lawyer is arguing that this settlement should include a portion of her shareholding in the family firm. Her brothers are firmly against the idea, and this is a source of tension between the siblings.

The five children [F, G, H, I, and J] who currently comprise the *third generation* are still at school. The two oldest will enter university in the next couple of years, although it is not yet clear where they will study. None is as yet a shareholder in the family firm, though there has been some discussion around the idea of establishing a trust from which the third generation will benefit. Their primary and secondary education has already been paid for by the money in a trust set up by their grandparents.

The needs of the three generations for advice and support are markedly different. The *first generation* has used the services of local accountancy and law firms to serve the business, and acted as the sole directors of the company until they judged their children were ready to take board positions [as E has shown no interest in the firm, she is a shareholder, not a director, and draws no salary from the business]. To manage their personal wealth, the founding couple have employed an independent financial advisor to assist them with planning and managing their investments. Their portfolio is a fairly conservative one, delivering a steady flow of dividends and modest capital growth. To purchase their properties, they have dealt directly with real estate agents, and they have made all the arrangements for their children's upbringing, such as private schooling, themselves. From time to time, they have employed help, mainly for childcare and household cleaning, but only ever on a temporary basis. If asked, the couple would describe themselves as thrifty and very conscious that their success is the product of hard work, robust health and a certain amount of good luck. Their main concessions to the enjoyment of their wealth are to spend six weeks in their Barbadian house over the English winter and to cruise for three weeks during the summer. Their circle of acquaintance remains very much the people they have known for most of their lives.

Life is very different for the *second generation*, who now manage the business. Twenty-five years on, the brothers have changed their professional advisors from local to international firms of lawyers and accountants [though not without some parental opposition]. The banking arrangements have changed as well. At the time of acquisition, subsidiaries continue to use their own historical banks and professional advisors, but there is a clear path to migration for each new purchase to become integrated into the back-office administration used by the parent company. A collection of businesses is gradually becoming a corporation. The bankers the two siblings deal with are now in head office positions in London, New York, and Singapore, and extend to specialists in mergers and acquisitions.

One of the brothers has also strengthened ties with the business school where he took his MBA, which runs programmes for family businesses. The firm offers internships for the school's students each year, involving placements at companies within the groups. The aim is to turn promising students into ambassadors for the firm, with offers of employment for those whose internship is noticeably successful. The two brothers are also planning to attend a week-long Family Business Programme at the same business school, and to include their sister in this. [Their parents have declined to participate.] It has become increasingly clear to the second generation that this family business is now a complex, multinational entity which plays in a completely different league from the one in which their parents began. The directors not only need to think more strategically about the future of the business, but also to take account of the interplay between ownership, management and family: how should the next generation be prepared in readiness to enter the family firm, assuming they wish to?

On the domestic front, things also look very different. The dividends from the business that accrue to the three children who have shares in the company are invested in funds managed by a multi-family office,[4] administered by an international private bank. Not unusually, this bank also looks after the private banking needs of all three siblings. Between them, the three siblings and their spouses own six properties, three main residences and three holiday apartments: two seaside villas and a mountain chalet. They use the services of concierge companies to maintain and decorate all these properties, and specialist agencies to let the holiday properties when not in use by the families. All three families have employed nannies and other full-time domestic help. In addition, they also each retain their own professional advisors to deal with their family's tax affairs and other liabilities, as these vary between jurisdictions.

Their social circle looks very different as well. The brothers' friends are drawn from the same class of the mobile, internationally wealthy; their children attend the same schools, they sail and ski together at the same resorts in Europe and North America. Their sister divides her leisure time between her medical colleagues and socialising with Italian friends who enjoy similar incomes. In truth, she does not need to work, but does so because she enjoys practising medicine.

The third-generation cousins are relatively close and see quite a lot of each other during the school holidays, enjoying the same sports. They have wanted for nothing, and it would be an understatement to describe their upbringing as a privileged one. Their friends are all drawn from the same moneyed circles. It is still too soon to say which, if any, will want to pursue a career in the family business; neither the family nor the firm has any settled policies on the employment of family members. This is one of the many issues which the second generation hopes to resolve by attending the business school's Family Business Programme.

Our imaginary case study is fictional, but representative. Within the space of a few decades, an entity that began life as an idea discussed around a kitchen table has grown into a multinational group of businesses that employs more than a thousand people in multiple countries. Everything has changed: the character of the business has altered radically, it has moved from local to global, and the family has been translated into the ranks of the internationally rich. If they choose wisely, the upcoming generation may never actually have to earn their own living, which raises another set of questions entirely.

There are risks associated with any business, but because the business that funds the family's lifestyle is so much more valuable, those risks are proportionately greater. The impending divorce demanded by E's estranged husband has brought some of them into sharp relief. For example, until now, the share structure of the business is relatively straightforward: all shareholders hold the same class of shares with equal voting rights. Is it time to separate the right to receive dividends from the right to decide company policy? If some shares are to pass outside the "blood" family, perhaps it makes sense to create two classes of share to protect the original shareholders from any future hostilities or serious disagreements. Or maybe a new holding company needs to be formed to control the family business, with ownership vested in the shareholders who actually manage the business? That would certainly suit the interests of siblings C and D, but could sister E be persuaded to agree? And even if she does, what guarantees or protections might she ask for in return to protect the interests of both herself and her son or any future children if she decides to re-marry?

What our case illustrates, moreover, is that the "life-support" system on which the family now depends has also changed dramatically. The lifestyle enjoyed by the first generation was less luxurious, but also infinitely less complicated: their descendants are surrounded by the entourage of experts and professionals depicted in the graphic above. The purpose of this third chapter of the book is to delineate the roles which they play in the lives of this expanding group of ultra-rich clans.

Business Schools

The siblings in our fictional case study have instructed their firm of London lawyers to review the business's current ownership arrangements and suggest solutions to the predicaments identified, while they attend the Family Business Programme. The brothers are hopeful that participation will shed additional light on this and other matters which they haven't even thought about yet. They're hoping to come away with a roadmap laying out how to future-proof the firm's continuing existence and safeguard family harmony at the same time.

The claim to have founded the world's first business school is made by the French. In 1819, the Ecole de Paris de Commerce was created, known now as ESCP Business School, modelled on the system of grandes écoles that arose at the tail end of the

French Revolution. It was American universities, however, which seized upon the idea and popularised the notion of business education as a formal process, modelling themselves to a large extent on collegiate law schools. Although the best-known, Harvard was not actually the first[5] US business school; it has probably played the most significant part in promoting the concept of business as a body of knowledge to be acquired prior to entry into industry or commerce. Through most of the 20th century, the prime role of business schools in the US and elsewhere, as they saw it, was to prepare ambitious men and women for successful careers in large corporations, banks, and management consultancies. Faculty teaching and research was very largely directed to this end.

In the 1970s, a rising star in the ranks of Harvard Business School PhD students concluded that a significant element of the US economy was underserved by the country's business schools, and decided to do something about it. Professor John A. Davis, as he now is, can rightly be regarded as the godfather of family business education. He had spotted that family enterprises had a number of unique features and that conventional business education failed to take account of these. Families faced all the challenges of managing a "regular" corporation and also a different set of challenges arising from the dynamics within the family and the interplay between the family and the business. Among the most significant are:

- managing and resolving business disagreements while preserving family harmony
- planning for inter-generational succession
- managing inter-generational succession
- decisions on whether non-family members should assume board positions or be granted share ownership
- determining rules for compensating family members as managers within the business and as owners of the business
- setting criteria for entry into the business of the next generation and the rules for their progression within the business
- defining the roles and rights of spouses and ex-spouses
- determining the conditions for, and process of, selling part or all of the business

A failure on any one of these fronts could jeopardise both the business and the harmonious workings of the family. More to the point, these potential points of friction, if left unresolved, become ever more intractable as the business descends through the generations.

Under the supervision of Professor Renato Tagiuri, Davis developed what has now become the standard teaching and consultancy tool for mapping the relationship between family business management and ownership: the Three-Circle model, as shown below. It was published in Davis's doctoral dissertation and was the first real systematic representation of the dynamics that govern this relationship.

Davis's Three-Circle Model

Like many models developed at business schools, it takes a while to absorb. The principle, however, is simple. Family, business and ownership intersect in various ways, and the model captures and defines all possible roles which those involved with any one family business can play. Not every family business will feature all such roles, but as a business expands over time and through the generations the genius of the model is that it can accommodate all sizes and permutations of a business managed and/or owned by a family.

Moving clockwise, the actors in *segment 1* are shareholders who play no active role in the management of the business – passive shareholders, if you like – and who are not members of the family. In our fictional case study, E's

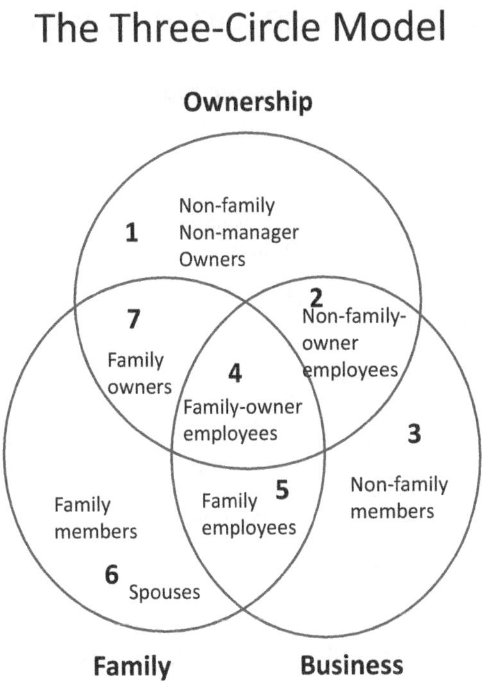

Figure 3.2 The Three-Circle model: *Developed by the author, based on the work of Professor John A. Davis*

soon-to-be-divorced husband may fall into this grouping if he succeeds in gaining a shareholding in the family business as part of the settlement.

Into *segment 2* fit company employees who own shares but are not members of the family: these might typically be loyal, long-serving members of staff whom the family wish to reward with a small stake in the firm [perhaps through a share-ownership scheme]; or new employees whom the directors want to attract through offering a stake as part of their employment package. Our fictitious company has so far not made any such offers.

In *segment 3* are the bulk of the workforce, who hold no shares in the company currently or through future entitlements.

Segment 4, at the intersection of the three circles, contains the family members who are both owners and managers of the company. In our case study, these are the two brothers.

In *segment 5*, we find family members who work in the firm but have no ownership stake. In our case study, we have no such actors as yet, although generation three may fall into that category at some stage in the future.

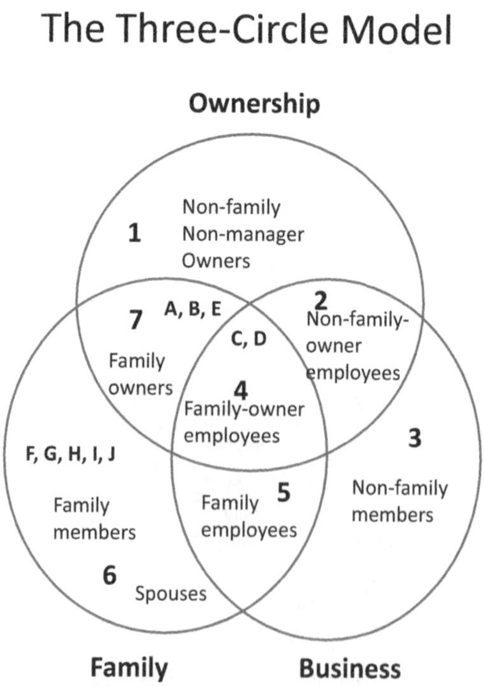

Figure 3.3 The Three-Circle model as applied to our example

Segment 6 contains family members who neither work in the firm nor have a share in it. These are typically spouses and young children, as in our case.

And finally, in *segment 7*, are family owners who play no part in the running of the company, such as sibling E in the case. In large, mature multi-generational family businesses, these often form the largest ownership group: each descendant has a relatively small shareholding, but they are many in number.

You can see above how our fictional family maps onto the Three-Circle model:

How the Family Fits

Our family members occupy four of the segments:

- E's soon-to-be ex-spouse, if his lawyer's demands are successful, will occupy *segment 1*, as a part-owner of the business but no longer a member of the family
- C and D are right at the core in *segment 4* as owners, managers and controlling shareholders
- *Segment* 6 is the most populous, containing third-generation F, G, H, I, and J, plus their mothers as spouses of C and D
- A, B, who are now retired, and E occupy *segment 7*, as family members who own shares but have no involvement in management

The diagramme is a snapshot of things as they stand, or are likely to stand in the near future. There is also some room for interpretation or debate as time goes on; for example, are spouses to be considered fully fledged members of the family with no limit on their entitlements to take employment in the firm or own shares? If so, should there be legal agreements in place that allow the company or other family members to buy back shares from spouses on the divorce or death of a family shareholder [such as C or D]? Depending on the view taken by the family, spouses might at some future point transition from segment 6 to segment 7, and as they come into their inheritance, third-generation family members [and their descendants] will certainly move into other segments.

Differing Generational Perspectives

The model is an excellent tool for flushing out whether the current arrangements – which have often evolved as much by chance as by design – are fit for purpose, or a source of tension and discord. Our case study is a fairly rudimentary one, in that the business is still only in the hands of the second generation and the family numbers are small, but it highlights the varying needs and expectations of the different stakeholders.

First-generation A and B are no longer dependent on the business for their financial needs. However, they will almost certainly see it as their legacy and want it properly stewarded by their children – the second generation – in the interests of their grandchildren, the third generation. They may well also have strong bonds with long-serving employees and want their interests to be protected as well. They are no longer directors, but have influence over the company so long as they retain shares, plus the influence derived from their role as parents.

Second-generation C and D have a direct financial interest in the business. They rely on it for employment and the cash generated by dividends, which funds their lifestyles. It is also their chosen career path, and affords them status as well as income. At some point, the income produced by their investments will equal the salaries they currently receive, but that point has not yet been reached. Several times over the years, the company has been approached by prospective buyers, but the offers have not been enough to tempt them to sell. While the two brothers agree there is still more value to be created, C, by nature a deal-maker, has a figure in mind at which he would be prepared to sell. D is resistant to the idea, as his whole professional life is wrapped up in the business. He has no idea what he would do without it. This divergence is a source of some, largely unspoken, tension between the two.

Second-generation E, their sister, takes no active interest in the firm. Her shares provide her with the means to enjoy a standard of living she could otherwise never afford. As a result of the current messy divorce proceedings, she is willing to trade a portion of her shares to guarantee primary custody of her son: it's not a question of principle, but of how much. That's for the lawyers to argue over, and is likely to cause friction with her brothers. However, she remains close to her parents and has a better understanding than her brothers have of the emotional ownership of the firm which they still retain.

Third-generation F, G, H, I, and J have differing levels of awareness of the significance of the business, in direct proportion to their ages. The two eldest, F and G, are very conscious that they owe their good fortune to the family firm; the younger cousins, not so much so. The parents have discussed in general terms that the next generation should be prepared for their future roles as owners and possibly managers, but no concrete plans have yet been made. At this stage in the lives of the rising generation, the lifestyle which the family business provides is more important than attachment to the firm.

Even this cursory analysis hints at the topics that are central to the stuff of drama: power, influence, money, emotional commitment, divergent goals, sibling ambitions, and potential rivalries. Our case study features only one marital breakdown. Imagine the potential for the amplification of conflict in real-life dynasties such as the Murdoch family, where the 94-year-old patriarch has recently embarked on his fifth marriage, to the former mother-in-law of Roman Abramovich. From his marriages, Rupert Murdoch [the world's 71st richest person according to Forbes magazine] has six children and the rivalry between the sons from his second marriage, Lachlan and James, has been well-publicised. The succession to Rupert's position as Chairman of both Fox and News Corporation was finally decided in Lachlan's favour in 2023. Controversy still continues to dog the family. At the time of writing, the family remains embroiled in a legal dispute in Nevada, where, against the wishes of James, Lachlan and Prudence [a daughter by his first marriage], Rupert is trying to overturn a family trust so that all his children will benefit equally from his estate.[6]

Business Schools Today

In Figure 3.1 earlier in this chapter describing the eco-system of support surrounding wealthy family businesses/business families, business schools were positioned to straddle each side: supporting both families *and* their business interests. In the half-century or so since Professor John A. Davis began his research into the unique features of family businesses, first at Harvard and later at the Massachusetts Institute of Technology [MIT], the number of programmes delivered by these institutions has exploded. They tend to address a number of core issues: the management of succession, preparing the next generation to assume the reins, reconciling and aligning shareholder and stakeholder interests, the responsibilities of families to their communities, and so forth. Dozens of US schools now offer such courses, and business schools elsewhere in the world have followed in their path. The focus ranges from courses geared to managing family money to programmes that concentrate more on understanding family dynamics and resolving tensions. For 25 years, the Wharton School at the University of Pennsylvania has hosted a week-long Private Wealth Management Programme, in association with publisher Campden Wealth and the Institute for Private Investors. Its aim is to demystify the process of investment, to enable newly enriched families to have informed conversations with wealth management professionals or to take the management of their fortunes into their own hands.

Among Europe's top business schools, Insead's Wendel International Centre for Family Enterprises, founded in 1997, offers programmes that address family business sustainability and inter-generational longevity; IMD's Global Family

Business Centre in Lausanne has been doing much the same for 30 years. Cambridge University's Family Business Leadership Programme and Lancaster University's Family Business Excellence Programme are prominent in this field in the UK.

In many cases, the ties between individual families and the business schools are close: Insead's Wendel Centre, for instance, is supported by France's de Wendel family, whose multi-generational firm has been in business since the 18th century. One of IMD's Professorial Chairs in Family Business is funded by the Schmidheiny family, whose fortune derives from materials for the construction industry, and the school's annual Global Family Business Award was for many years supported by the private, family-owned bank Lombard Odier. Top business schools also provide numerous executive education programmes designed to address the broader interests of all types of commercial organisation, where family business owners can find themselves sitting next to their non-family peers across all sectors, grappling with similar issues.

Family Offices[7]

Family office describes a dedicated investment entity that deals solely with managing family wealth. Family offices come in two forms: single- and multi-family offices. The choice of type depends very largely on how much investible money the family has.

Chapter 1 described how wealthy Roman families delegated the management of their assets to trusted servants, and emperors to their freed slaves [freedmen]. As far as we can tell, the modern variant of this concept first came into existence in the second half of the 19th century, as industrialisation started to create vast fortunes not tied to ruling houses. Rich European families entrusted stewardship of their wealth to nascent private banks such as Rothschilds: the newly rich of the New World pioneered the idea of appointing their own dedicated wealth managers to invest the surpluses produced by their enormous commercial success. By all accounts, oil magnate John D. Rockefeller was first out of the traps. He hired a certain Frederick Gates to create a Private Office that would manage both the family's commercial investments and its philanthropic activities. The Rockefeller assets were so extensive that in no time the office was fully staffed and the world's first single-family office was born. With the American economy roaring ahead in the 1860s and 1870s, it was a golden age for unbridled capitalism: Rockefeller's Standard Oil controlled around 90% of US oil refining and distribution by the end of the 1870s. Its monopoly was eventually dismantled in the 20th century, but not before Rockefeller had become the richest man on earth – in fact, the dismantling led to him becoming even richer, as he now had shareholdings in multiple companies as opposed to just one. As a Harvard Business School case study puts it, with wealth on his death estimated at US$1.4 billion, his personal fortune equated to 1.5% of the country's GDP – making him by that metric "the richest individual in American business and economic history."[8]

In our case study, a family office service is provided by the private bank with which family members in the second-generation bank personally [the parents of the founding generation stick resolutely to their long-standing banking relationships]. Some private banks label this their Private Office. This potentially creates conflicts, since it is imperative that a family office act independently of the institution which manages the assets, in order to have the family's interests at heart. Nevertheless, this tension can happen. The generic term for this arrangement is multi-family office, or MFO. A team of fund managers within the bank devote themselves to managing the investment portfolios of a number of HNW families, whose investible assets per family exceeded a certain threshold. When I was acting as an advisor to one such bank in the 2000s, that threshold was set at £10 million. Today, it may well be twice that. JP Morgan sets the threshold at US$30 million, since it is assumed that this is a level at which the returns on the wealth [at, say, 5% per annum] enable further areas where a family office can help, such as structural planning, philanthropy, and estate planning.

Over time, our fictional family may decide to migrate to a single-family office [SFO], dealing solely with that family's investments, if they decide among themselves that their needs are very specific and cannot be accommodated by the MFO, and they have the assets to sustain it. An SFO will cost anywhere between US$500,000 and US$5 million per annum to maintain, inclusive of salaries, IT spend, and office rental, while an MFO would charge up to 1% per year of assets under management for its services. It therefore stands to reason that an SFO only becomes viable once the family wealth hits US$50 million or more. Our family will also have to meet a much higher bar in terms of assets under management, entrusted to their wealth managers: a recent article posted by Tharawat Magazine[9] suggested that at least £50 million was the going rate to justify the outlay.

An SFO and an MFO provide broadly similar services, some of which will be in-house and some of which will be outsourced [for example, compliance, and IT]. The team of asset managers will establish at the outset the balance between capital growth and the family's need for cash to fund their living expenses, and the family's appetite for risk. Stock markets, for instance, provide higher returns over the long term, while money held in government bonds can be more rapidly turned into cash. In line with the family's instructions, the managers will select a range of asset classes – such as property, shares, bonds, precious metals, fine art, vintage wines and so forth – and the geographic spread. Thus, the risk of too many eggs in a single basket is diversified. They will also decide the balance between investing directly or via intermediate funds, which have already chosen the assets and made their allocations. Higher potential rewards entail higher risks. So, for instance, investing directly in early-stage, privately held companies is inherently risky: if the businesses go bust, the investor is likely to lose most, if not all, of their money. On the other hand, if the business is wildly successful, then the early-stage investor stands to make returns of many hundreds of per cent, as did the venture funds backing Google and Facebook [now Meta] in their infancies.

After over a century, the wheel came full circle in 2018 when the Rockefeller family office opened its doors to other wealthy families by turning itself into Rockefeller Capital Management, a multi-family office to manage the wealth of outsiders.

A family office will not only be staffed by investment professionals. These will be supplemented by lawyers, accountants and specialists in what are known collectively as alternative assets. "Traditional" assets are investments such as shares, bonds and cash deposits – basically anything that is either cash or can be turned into cash at short notice. "Alternatives" cover investments such as art, fine wines, and spirits, cryptocurrencies, currency trading, hedge funds and venture capital companies investing in private firms: all assets whose value is inherently more volatile – hence riskier – and usually take longer to turn into cash: illiquid, in the jargon of investment. It might seem an odd term to apply to premier cru Bordeaux and single-malt whiskies, but high finance has a vernacular all of its own. And all these experts do not come cheap.

The Office of the Wealth Manager

Alexander Rupert von der Vellen is the founder and principal of Adamas Advisors, a niche family office currently based in Andorra and Dubai. After serving in the British Army, he pursued a career in finance, working for merchant and private banks in various countries before establishing Adamas Advisors in 2005. He describes his business as an unusual hybrid of multi- and single-family offices. "At the moment we have nine clients and assets under management of around $US5 billion," he says. "I have said the number of clients will never exceed ten. Beyond that, we simply could not deliver the level of personal service which is core to our ethos as a firm."

Multi-family offices are subject to a much tighter set of regulations than single-family ones, and quite rightly so in Alexander's opinion: "We deliberately operate as an SFO and do so with Chinese walls that protect our clients. We have, at the same time, some advantages of scale. The reason that family offices exist in such numbers as a service today can be traced directly to the financial events of the 2000s. Large banks that had previously offered structuring and tax optimisation advice, in addition to executing trades and creating investment vehicles such as trusts, simply found it was too risky and uneconomic to continue doing so [*vide* UBS scandal of 2007]. Family offices came in to fill the significant gap which was created by this exit from the advisory business, as private banks moved over to a transactional model. We advise primarily, but are also involved in the management of wealth. Our key advantage in the market is the ability to offer a level of responsiveness and agility that families want. My clients expect me to answer their calls and respond to their emails immediately – which is impossible if you're servicing 4,000 or so clients, as many larger providers are."

Alexander also has decided opinions on the differences between family offices in North America and those in Europe. "The US family office-client relationship is much more of a professional business one. As an example, an American family office would expect an investing client to disclose their tax affairs, to understand their financial position, and a US client would consider that normal. In Germany, by contrast, the reaction would be "Why do you want to know that? It's a private matter."

In Europe, the relationship is very much more personal. One of the things I am most proud of is that I am a godparent to the children of three of the families my company looks after. That's how I measure my success.

"There are other cultural differences, too. In the States, most family offices are more or less private equity operations, seeking out the next big new technology or idea. That reflects the environment they operate in – the vast majority of VC and PE investment worldwide still happens in the US – as well as the expectations of the family investor. Elsewhere, the investment preferences are for safer bets. In the Middle East and Eastern Europe, there is a similarly strong preference for building trusted personal relationships first and worrying about business performance afterwards. In a highly volatile economic environment like Russia, a client will seek above all to secure their financial position and protect their family's well-being: if you have to carouse until the small hours to create that bond of trust, so be it!"

For now and in the future, Alexander maintains that the quality of the personal relationship is Adamas's most important asset. "I can buy in the technical expertise I need, in crypto, blockchain, whatever new asset classes are emerging. What sets us apart is experience accrued over many years and the fact that we answer our calls promptly!"

Source: In conversation with the author.

The primary aim of any family office is to preserve and enhance the wealth of those who participate in it. Reverting to our fictional family business, let's assume that after 30 years of operations from start-up, the second generation has now amassed between them the £20 million of investible assets that make it viable to take advantage of their private bank's multi-family office. The initial target agreed with the fund managers is that their £20 million should grow by 5% annually net of fees. The three siblings [the parents do not participate] agree among themselves that all the returns should be reinvested, as they can cover their day-to-day expenses from salaries – in the case of the brothers – and dividends paid out of the business's trading profits. At the end of year one, assuming the 5% target is achieved, that £20 million is now £21 million. Invoking our old friend, the Rule of 72, after 14 years and a few months that initial £20 million should have doubled to £40 million, assuming that the average annual rate of growth stays steady at 5%. If the fund managers exceed their target, the fund doubles faster, and if the average rate of return does worse it takes longer.

It's a simplified example, of course, that doesn't take account of the two great eroders of cumulating wealth, inflation and taxation. So let's also assume that our fund managers are very competent and have access to some smart lawyers and accountants, and that those two factors are minimised. It might also be the case that the family members agree to pay a proportion of their dividends into the fund if the cash yielded by the business allows them to do so. Thus, the snowball gets even bigger as it rolls, and so do the returns. If that average annual rate of return is better than expected, at 7%, the fund reaches £40 million in a little over ten years. Through patience and careful stewardship of their wealth, the family has progressed within two generations from start-up to serious wealth.

The growth in family offices in recent years has been phenomenal, yet another proxy indicator of the worldwide rise in wealthy families. According to data collection specialists Prequin,[10] their numbers grew more than three times between 2019 and 2023. Worldwide, these offices in 2023 exceeded 4,500 in total, with the majority being MFOs. However, the split is only about 60:40 in their favour, with the balancing 40% of SFOs another indicator of the rise in the ranks of ultra-rich clans.

> *One phenomenon impacting both the creation of new family offices and their investment strategies is the great wealth transfer, which is expected to make Millennials*[11] *the richest generation in American history,*" noted Alex Murray, vice president, and Prequin's head of real estate assets and research insights. "*An ageing population means more family offices are transferred to the next generation – and this demographic shift is happening across the world. With this demographic change comes a shift in focus for family offices, from wealth creation to wealth retention.*

This transfer of wealth is the main theme of Chapter 4.

The Prequin report breaks down the geographic spread by North America/Europe/Asia-Pacific, and the rest of the world. The growth in the number of family offices is fastest in the rest of the world, at a yearly average of 31%, while North American family offices still lead the field in the value of assets under management. Offices of both sorts also tend to cluster around hubs by region: London, Paris, Zurich in Europe, for example, the major cities on each coast in the US, Dubai in the UAE, Singapore in the Far East and in Shanghai, China's main commercial centre. The phenomenon has attracted an enormous interest from those institutions that like to follow the money. Wealth Briefing observes, a little testily, that "*The business of producing reports and surveys about family offices is becoming crowded, potentially leading to a law of diminishing returns in their impact.*" The editor goes on to list a dozen recent reports [including the Prequin report] produced by assorted banks, fund managers and management consultancies. It appears everyone is getting in on the act.

Global consultancy Deloitte, on the other hand, puts an even higher figure on the number of family offices and confirms their exceptional rate of growth. The firm's *Family Office September 2024 Survey* reports a current worldwide total of 8,030 single-family offices alone, an increase in their number of almost a third in five years. A breakdown of that growth by region presents the following picture [see overleaf]:
The survey is based on feedback from 354 single-family offices worldwide [presumably supplemented with desk research], conducted between September and December 2023. Of this sample, the average value *per family* of assets under management [or AUM, as the industry terms it] is US$2 billion, and the average wealth per family is US$3.8 billion [these families clearly don't put all

Table 3.1 Worldwide growth in single-family offices by region

Date	*2019*	*2024*	*Rate of increase**	*2025 [projected]*	*2030 [projected]*	*Rate of increase***
North America	2,210	3,180	*31%*	3,550	4,190	*24%*
Europe	1,680	2,020	*20%*	2,290	2,650	*24%*
Asia-Pacific	1,790	2,290	*28%*	2,600	3,200	*35%*
Middle East	250	290	*16%*	310	350	*17%*
South America	150	190	*27%*	210	240	*21%*
Africa	50	60	*20%*	70	90	*50%*
Global	**6,130**	**8,030**	**31%**	**9,030**	**10,720**	**25%**

* between 2019 and 2024 **between 2024 and 2030 [projected]

Source: Deloitte Global Family Office survey, recompiled by the author.

their eggs in one basket, no matter how good their family fund managers]. The Deloitte report puts the total value of assets managed by family offices worldwide at US$3.1 trillion – that's US$3,100 billion – and the totality of wealth owned by families that use these offices at US$5.5 trillion. These are estimates, of course, based at least partly on sampling and extrapolation. Even if they are out by 10–15%, the sums are enormous. For context, the GDP of the UK economy was £2.3 trillion in 2023, say US$2.9 trillion more or less, depending on exchange rate fluctuations. The total value of assets under management held by SFOs thus exceeds the aggregate value of goods and services the UK produces annually, and the total wealth of the families who use these offices greatly exceeds it.

As you might expect, given the historical proliferation of wealth in the United States, between 2019 and 2024 the pace of SFO growth at 31% was fastest in North America. Growth in Europe is more sluggish and outpaced by Asia-Pacific, while other regions grow more slowly from a much lower base: the Middle East, for example, has both a relatively small population compared with either Europe or North America, and family wealth is heavily concentrated in a tiny fraction of households. Relatively speaking, Africa lags far behind.

If the Deloitte projections as shown in the table above are even broadly correct, the growth in ultra-rich family wealth between now and 2030 is staggering: the number of single-family offices is, as already noted, a proxy indicator. In North America, their numbers will grow by almost a quarter, as they will do in Europe. Their numbers in Asia-Pacific already exceed those of Europe, and so will the expected rate of growth, at 35%. Offices in the Middle East are predicted to grow by 17%, and those in South America and Africa are to grow significantly, albeit from a lower base. The Deloitte survey also estimates US$ 2030 numbers for SFO AUM and total family wealth of those who use them, of US$5.4 trillion and $US9.5 trillion respectively.

The West, in the form of Europe and North America, will still head the global number of single-family offices [64%], but those in Asia-Pacific and the Middle East are rapidly closing the gap.

Concierge Services: Your Wish Is My Pay-Cheque

To say that the rich have always employed servants is something of a statement of the obvious. For many people, what is the point of doing something yourself if you can pay someone else to do it for you? What is more interesting, however, is the transformation of the way in which these services are bought and provided.

The defining moment can most credibly be dated to the year 2000 when Quintessentially opened its doors for business. Founded by a trio of smart young men about town [one of them the nephew of the present Queen of the United Kingdom], it started in a small way and then grew rapidly. Today, the Quintessentially Group has a turnover of around £50 million and 60 offices worldwide. It offers bespoke luxury services to a clientele that can afford its membership fees. On this subject, its website is, shall we say, coy. If you have to ask, you probably cannot afford it. Subscription varies depending on which services you wish to purchase and where you wish to use them. Press coverage reported that a UK-only annual membership in 2017 cost €15,000. No doubt that has risen with inflation. If you want the full works, the platinum service 24 hours a day, seven days a week, anywhere in the world, you are looking at six figures. Quintessentially can arrange every aspect of your life: travel and holiday bookings, restaurant reservations, concert tickets, buying, selling or renting property, advising on and securing places at the best schools, organising parties and events … the list goes on. And yes, that includes recruiting household staff as well.

Up until the time of the company's foundation, these services could already be bought by those in the know: the concierge concept, after all, was pioneered by the grand hotels of the world's great cities, whose front desk staff held – and still hold – an invaluable black book of contacts. Specialist agencies, of the type that advertised their services in venerable publications like *The Lady* [now sadly extinct], were recruiting butlers and nannies long before Quintessentially was founded, and continue to do so. What Ben Elliott and his well-connected co-founders spotted was that the new wave of global money washing up in London, New York and Paris craved access, but lacked the contacts to get it. The rise of celebrity culture was a happy coincidence. New money was desperate to rub shoulders with the powerful and the famous. A private dinner in a royal residence? Elton John or Bryan Ferry performing at your daughter's wedding in the Seychelles? If money is really no object, there's almost always a way, provided you know the right people.

The defining difference between the "old money" way of doing things and that of the newly wealthy is its transactional nature. Forget Downton Abbey, benevolent paternalism and a lifetime's career moving up the ranks in a stately household. Today's staff are hired and fired through a "facilitator" who can turn on a sixpence. They will staff your residence, crew your yacht, cater for your chalet, and provide round-the-clock security from the ranks of ex-special forces personnel. [It is not uncommon, for instance, for the more paranoid leading families of the Middle East to dismiss their existing security detail and hire a new one every three or six months.] It's just business, and the facilitation services they use rest entirely on contacts. Concierge, or lifestyle management companies, as they like to call themselves, do not themselves directly employ a vast army of staff with all the necessary professional skills. Their employees simply maintain an enormous database of the right people available at the right price at a moment's notice.

Like all innovators, Quintessentially has spawned its share of imitators and competitors. The *Money* section of the Daily Telegraph, 26 October 2024, profiled a number of them based out of London: S2, Calder & Co, Velocity Black, and BHB Private. S2 were less shy about the price of membership: for a couple, the annual fee works out at £108,000, including VAT. For that, the firm's owners maintain their service is actually good value for money, comparable to the costs of hiring a top-of-the-range Personal Assistant. No client whim appears too bizarre: according to *The Telegraph*, members who were travelling to Colombia some time ago were able to meet a surviving family members of the late drug baron Pablo Escobar, to hear their version of events.

However, S2 failed to obtain for a client a special audience with Taylor Swift when she was touring the UK. That privilege was reserved for the Prince of Wales.

Another highly prized service offered by several concierge companies is the fast-tracking of membership applications to fashionable clubs. The best-known of these is probably Soho House, originating in London and now with over 40 locations worldwide. Founded just five years before Quintessentially, Soho House also benefited from the economic tailwinds of the 2000s. As its name suggests, it was aimed initially at the creative fraternity working in London's West End – in media companies, fashion and the arts. Such was its success, others working in less hip sectors like finance clamoured to join, a phenomenon similar to the way that once-Bohemian city districts like Greenwich Village and Shoreditch have been colonised by those wishing to live a little – but not too much – on the edge. A victim of its own eminence, under pressure from long-standing members, Soho House has been forced to close application lists at its main clubhouses in London, New York and Los Angeles. I write these words a few miles from its Somerset outpost, Babington House, where, throughout the school holidays, multi-generational families of the rich and famous swim in its pools and play on its tennis and padel courts. Photography is strictly forbidden. In the summer, it musters its own cricket team, and throughout the year it hosts weddings and other special events. If you have £40,000 or £50,000 to spare, you can take over the entire place for a weekend.

In the sections that follow, we take a closer look at the sorts of service providers who are likely to feature in the black books of concierge companies.

Childcare and School Selection

Who can forget Mary Poppins? From the book written by P.J. Travers in 1934, Walt Disney made one of his corporation's best-known and best-loved movies. It made Julie Andrews an international star and gave the world the least-convincing cockney accent of all time in the form of Dick Van Dyke's chimney-sweep Bert.

For an entire regiment of real-life Mary Poppinses, one need look no further than Bath-based Norland College. Since 1892, this institution has provided the British-trained nannies who have reared the children of families across the world. The founder, Emily Ward, was part of the great wave of Victorian reformers and advocates of social change and improvement, of which the philanthropy movement discussed in Chapter 1 was a branch. Ward was much influenced by the ideas of the German educationalist Friedrich Fröbel, pioneer of the kindergarten or children's nursery. Trained initially as a teacher, she opened what was then the Norland Institute in Norland Square, Notting Hill. Until that time, the early years' care of the children of the British upper and middle classes was delegated almost exclusively to their servants. In many cases, such care as there was, was harsh to the point of being brutal, and left to the whims and caprice of those in charge of their charges. In *The Rise and Fall of the British Nanny*,[12] Jonathan Gathorne-Hardy describes horror tales experienced by some notable products of a Victorian upbringing, such as Lord Curzon, later Viceroy of India, and Winston Churchill.

Ward intended to put a stop to that. Her vision was to create a cadre of highly trained professionals, informed by scientific principles and a profound understanding of best practice in infant and toddler development. This new breed of nursery nurses, as they were first called, would be independent young women to be treated not as servants, nor as members of the family, but as members of a new social order between the two. Ward succeeded, and her legacy survives her.

Gathorne-Hardy's eminently readable and well-researched book was first published in 1972. His choice of title was perhaps influenced by the grim decade in which he wrote it, a time of British economic crisis and much industrial strife, embodying a pervading sense of national decline. The book's title was retained for the second edition, but history has proved the author prematurely pessimistic. Far from being in decline, the British Norland-trained nanny is resurgent and in high demand.

At this point, I should declare a personal interest, as the father of two Norland nannies. However, this has given me a useful vantage point, since my daughters were trained 12 years apart: the first graduated in 2013, the second obtained her Norland Diploma in 2025. In that time, the course has lengthened from two years to three, but much else has stayed the same – the mastery of cooking, for example, an understanding of the theories of early years' development, the training in martial arts, defensive driving techniques gained on the skidpans of the Castle Combe circuit. In the spirit of Mary Poppins, the modern nanny comes equipped for all circumstances and, as she[13] will tell you, she is much, much more than an au pair. The biggest change is in the intake: numbers have more or less quadrupled in the last 15 years, to meet demand. Norland College has been forced to expand into additional premises in Bath. It's another indicator of the growth in families with serious means.

To qualify fully, each Norlander has to spend a year gaining practical experience, working with a family. For purposes of supervision, they must remain in the UK. At the end of it all, successful graduates receive both a bachelor's degree and Norland's own Diploma. And then they are free to join families across the world. Other nanny-training colleges have come and gone, but Norland – unusually for an educational institution – remains unchallenged in its prestige and brand recognition. Many families seeking a nanny will specifically request a Norlander, and their services command a hefty premium. On graduating, the alumnae can confidently expect a starting salary today of at least £40,000, living in a household. It is not unheard of for those with significant experience, say five years at a minimum, to earn US$250,000 in New York or Los Angeles. And the self-contained nanny flat comes as part of the package.

Childcare for the ultra-rich family commences even earlier than infancy. Mayfair specialists ESB Consulting will attend the birth of a child at one of London's top private hospitals, or the private sections of major NHS hospitals like the Lindo Wing at St Mary's. Within hours of birth, ESB will register your child for a place at a number of London's select nurseries and initiate the application process for registering for the city's top private pre-preparatory and preparatory schools. Even prior to the birth, such consultancies offer advice on choosing gynaecologists and the hospitals where they practise. Throughout pregnancy their own variety of concierge services will assist in furnishing and decorating the nursery, selecting private midwives, maternity nurses, nannies, and finding sleep consultants to settle baby into a routine. Private midwives, doulas and night nurses do promote their own services, of course, but consultancies offer a one-stop service which many families find more convenient.

At every stage of a child's development, a plethora of service providers exists to support this clientele. A nanny will usually cease childcare beyond the age of 5 or 6, although some families will retain their services to deliver and collect children throughout the years of school attendance. Beyond that point, the primary responsibility rests with the school – and sometimes with a private tutor – and if your child is unable to attend the prestigious school of your choice in London, these schools will come increasingly to you. For many years, "international" schools have operated in places popular with wealthy expatriates/tax exiles, or relocated professionals and multinational company executives. You can find them in Switzerland, Monaco, France [there is one, for instance, in Fontainebleau near Paris, which educates many of the children of Insead's faculty], and elsewhere in Europe. They teach mainly in English and offer a curriculum which is either broadly based and international or replicates the education of a specific country: such as the American School in St John's Wood, for instance, which does as the name implies, and the Lycée Français Charles de Gaulle de Londres in South Kensington [there are offshoots in Turkey and Africa as well], serving the French expatriate community in west London, which numbers many thousands. King's College Wimbledon is in partnership with the International School of Monaco, and some of its peers have begun to look to North America: Wellington College has opened its doors in San Francisco, and Harrow is following suit in New York, both campuses branded as "International."

Truly, the real phenomenon in global private education has been the worldwide export of English-language and specifically British education. Website *Which School Advisor* [whichschooladvisor.com] lists 22 British schools which have created affiliates abroad. Dulwich College pioneered the trend with the opening of Dulwich College Shanghai in 2003, and under the Dulwich College International brand has schools in Seoul and Singapore, as well as a second in Shanghai and elsewhere in China. Harrow Beijing opened in 2005, and more British schools have followed: for instance, King's College Wimbledon has two, in Wuxi and Hangzhou. In Singapore, you will find not just Dulwich but an offshoot of The Perse [a Cambridge school], Brighton College, and the North London Collegiate School, offering the IB [International Baccalaureate]. In Thailand, you will find international versions of Brighton and Harrow again, and also Rugby, Bromsgrove, Shrewsbury, Wellington College, as well as King's College Wimbledon. In Hong Kong, it's once again Harrow and Shrewsbury, but also Malvern College and the all-girls Wycombe Abbey. Uppingham appears to be in a lengthy process of establishing a presence in Vietnam, while Sir Keir Starmer's alma mater, Reigate Grammar, has already set up shop in Hanoi. In Japan, you will find an offshoot of Rugby, and in Kazakhstan an extension of Charterhouse is planned for 2026.

It is in the Arabian Peninsula that English-language private education has really taken hold. In Dubai, another old grammar school that is now independent of the state, the Royal Grammar School Guildford, opened its campus in 2021. Brighton College has not one but two offshoots in Abu Dhabi, as well as a presence in Dubai, where it is joined by Kent College. Cranleigh has a school in Abu Dhabi, as does King's College Wimbledon, and Repton has three schools bearing its brand across the UAE. One of the world's largest providers of private education, GEMS[14] [Global Education Management Systems] operates numerous schools across the region, some under its own brand and others in association with leading British schools such as Wellington and Winchester. The emphasis again is on a Western-style education, the curricula generally following the British or the US patterns.

The business model used by these schools is typically a joint venture or franchise arrangement, the pedagogy delivered by teachers trained in their countries of origin and the commercial side managed by the local partner. The partner benefits from access to a prestigious brand, with all the history and tradition that implies, and the school from the expertise of people on the ground with local knowledge.[15] The fact that there is wide replication – single schools with multiple offshoots – suggests that scaling up is financially attractive: one back office can service multiple campuses. These schools and their facilities can also be constructed on the ground to modern standards without the high maintenance costs of operating in draughty listed buildings back home. From a financial perspective, there are benefits to the schools concerned: surpluses can be reinvested to grow the local business, or repatriated – subject to domestic legislation – to be used for investment in the parent institution, such as repairing the roofs, or for funding scholarships and other charitable works. The links to the mothership school vary. In some cases, these appear to be close; in others, more tenuous. To what extent a child attending Harrow School Beijing "went to Harrow" is an interesting question. But this proliferation of Western education certainly provides a springboard which ambitious parents can use to prepare their children for an elite university education in the West.

Private Tutoring

If school provision is insufficient in some way, families can always turn to a private tutor. This service has always existed in various forms and in the guise of different interventions at various stages of a child's education. Schoolteachers have a long tradition of supplementing their incomes by offering extra lessons out of hours. In Oxford, Cambridge, and London primarily, private tutorial colleges have flourished for decades, enabling students to resit their GCSEs or A levels and improve their chances of a place at the university of their choice. But today, what was a sideline or a niche activity is a seriously big industry, valued at between £6 billion and £7.5 billion in the UK alone, depending on which source you consult. The size is hard to know exactly, because it's an unregulated market. The demand is enormous and growing: it is estimated that there are 100,000 private tutors in the UK and that some 46% of parents in London make use of them. In 2013 The Tutors' Association was formed as a representative body cum trade association and is probably the most authoritative source of information: it claims to represent 50,000 tutors and has a large corporate membership. If you want to get into this, there are any number of published how-to guides. In 2014, the inevitable *Confessions of a Private Tutor*[16] appeared, a steamy romp through the personal services allegedly provided by the author. It's classified as fiction, but who knows?

The real money and associated perks lie in tutoring the children of the ultra-rich. Some idea of the opportunities available can be gleaned from the website of Tutors International.[17] In 2022, Matthew Knott published his own account of wandering into this profession more or less by accident: *A Class of Their Own: Adventures in Tutoring the Super-Rich*.[18] It's an extremely funny account of Knott's working for the internationally wealthy, time spent mainly in remedial teaching/babysitting of children who show little interest in learning, their tutors employed by parents who show not much interest in their children. It's a caricature, of course, but it does illustrate the glamour of a lifestyle spent travelling by private jet across continents at the command of those who pay for such services. The picture is confirmed by others: at the top of their game, the London tutors most in demand can command £350 per hour and earn upwards of £250,000 annually. They don't need to advertise: they work essentially on the basis of word-of-mouth, their names passed on from one client to another. Like Norland nannies, they occupy that ambiguous space between household staff and family members. As a general rule, at least in the United States, the further up the educational ladder you climb, the higher the rates. Thus, full-time tutoring for a child of high school age in the US reportedly pays half as well as preparing candidates for sitting the exams for law or business school. There are exceptions to this trend where there is high demand. Parents determined to get their children into the limited number of high-performing independent secondary schools in London will pay handsomely for coaching for the entrance tests.

Property

These children all require multiple roofs over their heads. Property is glamorous. Not merely the buying and selling of property, but the repair, restoration and refurbishment of property. It would be no exaggeration to say that the British in particular are obsessed with the subject, judging by the television schedules. Estate agents catering to the requirements of the rich and famous hunting for prime real estate in London, Los Angeles, and Dubai are the latest TV celebrities. Countless acres of newsprint and magazine articles, indeed, entire specialist publications, are devoted to the quest for property perfection.

The great majority of us are obliged to pay to see properties of historical and special interest. In 2023, the UK's National Trust welcomed 23.1 million paying visitors to its collection of over 500 historical national properties. Ultra-rich families do indeed pay, but not for a two-hour guided tour. They are there as proprietors for keeps, or until they get bored. Those great estates and townhouses which are not in the hands of The National Trust, English Heritage, or the aristocratic families that have managed to hold onto them are increasingly occupied by the globally rich. Take Scotland. The National Trust for Scotland may own 180,000 acres, but Danish billionaire Anders Holch Povlsen [fashion tycoon and sole owner of the business founded by his parents] possesses 220,000 acres, spread across 13 estates, making him one of the UK's biggest landowners. Sheikh Mohamed bin Rashid al-Maktoum owns 63,000 acres. The Duke of Buccleuch and Queensberry makes do with 200,000 acres, but these include land in England as well.

Our Fictional Family and Their Network of Support

Reverting to our fictional family, the husband and wife who founded the business will have used the services of estate agents to acquire the family house where they raised their children in the 1980s and 1990s. They were just like everyone else of their generation. And as growing wealth enabled them to trade up through the property market, so our couple traded up in terms of the estate agents they used. As in every market, different players have different audiences. For the next generation, however, there is an alternative option. As well as hiring a battery of housekeepers and nannies and maintaining their private club memberships, to purchase their family homes in London and New York they have engaged the services of property search agents.

Also known as buying agents, this new breed of property professional has grown in significance in recent decades. The pioneer in the London market was Stacks, founded in 1984, which was set up to act exclusively for property buyers – in New York, the phenomenon gathered momentum around the same time, although the service was provided mainly by real estate brokers. There seem to have been three main drivers. First, the mid-1980s economies of both the UK and the US were doing well. The Reagan administration stimulus to the American economy and Thatcher's wave of deregulation had put money in people's pockets, and there was a general sense of optimism. Property markets were booming, and entrepreneurship was in vogue. What was stopping you from getting rich by going into business on your own account? Second, there was dissatisfaction among some agents and property buyers over the service buyers were receiving from some of the established agents. The founder of London-based Mercury Homesearch, Jeremy McGivern, expresses it in forthright terms:

> Why did I found a residential property consultancy?
> The answer to this is simple – because I was deeply unhappy with the service and advice I was receiving as a buyer [of central London property].[19]

One person's problem is someone's opportunity.

Third, certainly in the UK, there is a conflict of interest inherent in the estate agency model. The seller instructs the agent, and the agent is duty-bound to attain the best price for his or her client. What the best price is exactly may be very hard to determine, but that's the obligation placed on the agent, who will present the property in the most attractive light possible. The prospective buyer is on the other side of the table. The agent's job, of course, is to coordinate what is, all too often, a fraught and complex transaction and that requires them to act as a broker between the parties. Nonetheless, at the end of the day, the seller pays the agent's fees.

Those estate agents which provide a tailored property search service, and the well-known firms at the top end mostly do, robustly disagree with this argument, maintaining that by operating separate departments they avoid any conflict of interest. In practice, search agents and estate agents tend to recognise that they need each other and co-existence is in both parties' best interest. All the same, many wealthy families would rather retain an independent search agent who acts solely on their behalf. The search agent will tell you that using their services has other advantages as well. A large number of sought-after properties in central London, perhaps as many as 40%, are sold off-market. They are never openly advertised or appear on estate agents' books. The sellers favour minimal publicity. Death, divorce and dramatic reversals of fortune are the main reasons for wanting a sale that creeps below the radar. Property search agents devote significant time to cultivating their connections with law firms that have advance notice of such events. Thus, they have a head start in the hunt. They will also argue that they frequently save the buyer the cost of their fees by securing a better purchasing price – many are, after all, former estate agents and experienced negotiators. In some instances, the search agents' circle of contacts extends to family consultants like ESB, who advise on school selection and entry preparation: invaluable if the family is seeking to buy in a location unfamiliar to them.

And then there is the financing of these properties. For most of us, buying a property means converting cash and other assets we have into equity as part of the way we finance the purchase. In the period before the invasion of Ukraine, interest rates in advanced economies were running at close to zero for a protracted period. Mortgage finance was cheap. For the ultra-rich, mortgage finance was extremely cheap. Lenders, particularly lenders who were keen to sell this clientele other services, were happy to lend money to asset-rich buyers on very favourable terms. A new breed of financial intermediary arose, who spotted the opportunity to broker lending deals based at least in part on using buyers' assets as collateral. Thus, if you wanted to acquire a house in Mayfair, Belgravia, or Kensington and were prepared to put up your art collection as surety, you could obtain a 100% mortgage at a cost that was considerably cheaper than renting – and still enjoy looking at your art collection, at least as long as the mortgage debt was serviced. If your income was sufficient to service a short-term repayment mortgage, this was a very efficient way to acquire an asset that was virtually guaranteed to increase in value far ahead of inflation. Once UK inflation really took off in 2022, however, this stratagem was off the table.

For the ultra-rich clans, property buying is not always about the grand town-house. Many maintain their main residence in their country of birth while acquiring a flat or apartment in the foreign capital[s] of their choice. Consider, for example, the residential blocks that now front the south bank of the Thames, marching all the way from Chelsea Bridge to Vauxhall and beyond. They house many thousands of apartments, a large number of which are occupied for only a few months of the year. The centrepiece is the refurbished power station, a vast new agglomeration of offices, apartments and a multi-storey shopping mall. Several times a year, I used to stay in one such apartment, as a guest of a family member who occupied a flat. From the balcony, you can look in one direction towards Battersea Park, and in another direction across the river towards the mansion blocks of Chelsea that occupy the northern bank. The contrast between these low- and mid-rise buildings, built mainly of red brick and unmistakably signalling "London," and the blocks on the south side could not be more marked. If I craned my neck, I could see a bridge upstream that marks the end of a street where I once lived, in one of these Edwardian mansion flats. The south-side apartment blocks, built in the last couple of decades, are constructed of concrete, glass and steel, in that uniform, international style you can find in Athens, Ankara, Dubai, Singapore, Hong Kong, and a dozen other cities where these design and architectural practices operate. In these enclaves, you could be pretty much anywhere. That is perhaps the attraction for the owners.

Occasionally, one block strives to be a little bolder, a little more distinctive than its neighbours and here and there among the apartment blocks, controlled by secure entrances, you will find a small supermarket and the odd hotel – it's very convenient for the West End. By far the most distinctive building is the gleaming new power station, which is an awesome edifice once you get close. It is a triumph of regeneration, with due attention paid to the building's history and heritage, influenced by Art Deco. The station once supplied a fifth of London's power and was decommissioned in 1983. After more than three decades of failed attempts by British[20] developers, its restoration and conversion were funded by a consortium of Malaysian investors. The renovation was completed in the autumn of 2022, and at its opening attracted, it is claimed, a quarter of a million visitors. On the site are some 4,000 new homes, of which 295 are in the power station itself. Apple has consolidated its new London headquarters here. At weekends, this new urban quarter's footpaths, restaurants, and shops are a hub for joggers, diners, and seekers of retail therapy. If you listen closely, you might hear a dozen languages spoken. Ambitious public artwork graces the riverside. Thirty-five years ago, when I lived across the river, Battersea was by and large an eyesore, crowned by the derelict power station. It has taken the vision and new financial muscle of South Asia to transform it.

In the basement of the block where I used to stay are two floors devoted to parking spaces for residents and visitors. There are rows upon rows of expensive metal, some of it covered by dustsheets. Most of the Porsches, Mercedes, and Ferraris appeared not to have been moved from one of my visits to the next. Some even bear Middle Eastern number-plates. Each block has a concierge desk, and "mine" has a small cinema that residents can book for their own use, for a small charge. The flats themselves are designed to make the best use of limited space, laid out as you would expect in a high-end, well-equipped apartment: clean lines, painted in neutral colours, all mod cons, ready to move into and lock up at a moment's notice. My daughter's landlady owns other flats in this and neighbouring buildings, purchased while she was working as an expat in Hong Kong. In fact, a very large number of the residents, perhaps the majority, are either expat Britons or overseas buyers. On the same floor live members of a charming Turkish family and an elderly couple who spend most of the year in the south of France. It's hard to know who lives there exactly, as the residents value their privacy and, in any case, are not present full-time. Family members come and go, some younger members using their apartments as a base while they take courses in the UK. They make ideal *pieds à terre*. The smallest and cheapest apartments rent for £3,000–£4,000 a month, if you can find one. If you were looking to buy, the prices start at around £1.25 million. It's central London, re-specified for the internationally mobile.

Professional Advisors

If a wealthy family is buying property for its own use in a city such as London, it will need the assistance of lawyers and accountants to prepare for and proceed with the transaction. Depending on the jurisdiction, residence requirements, and tax liabilities may well be complex. These professionals rely in turn on the expertise of niche publishers such as Globe Law and Business, who produce regular updates on the changing aspects of domiciliary arrangements across different countries. New governments enact changes in legislation that make it more or less attractive to existing and incoming international residents. Several southern European countries, such as Italy, Spain, Portugal, and Malta, have recently sought to encourage people of means and entrepreneurs to take up residence via tax breaks or relaxed visa requirements. There are, of course, strings attached, such as minimum investment requirements. Conversely, the UK has made it a little less attractive for wealthy overseas residents by amending the terms of the "non-dom" arrangements [allowing you to live in the country on very favourable tax terms].

The firms that specialise in these aspects of the law and tax showcase their expertise in the volumes produced by firms like Globe Law and Business [in *Business Families and Family Businesses*, for instance], and in the directories produced by publishers of magazines aimed at the ultra-rich family, such as Spears, Campden Family Business and Tharawat. Forbes produces a Top Advisors Directory for a North American audience. A number of glossies, such as Tatler, with its Tatler Address Book, produce lists that cover just about every kind of advisor which an ultra-rich family might have need of.

The mobility of the wealthy family is mirrored by the networks of those who support and advise them. Recent research[21] reports that 30% of family offices have multiple locations, partly for the convenience of their patrons and partly for proximity to the markets in which they invest. Many major US law firms, particularly those headquartered in New York, have a European presence, notably in London, gained either through acquisition, merger or informal alliances. To staff the rapid expansion of family offices worldwide, specialist recruitment firms like Agreus have sprung up: it has offices in New York, London, Dubai, and Singapore, and will find its clients a range of staff from executive PAs through to Chief Executives.

Family Enterprise Consultants

A new and fast-growing breed of consultants has also arisen. For years, the big consultancies such as McKinsey and the consultancy arms of the large accountancy firms like PwC have served the corporate and public sector markets, assisting large firms and governments to develop their strategies and restructure their operations. Family businesses have had their commercial interests represented by bodies such as the Family Firms Institute in the US and Family Business UK, based, as you might expect, in Britain. These organisations not only lobby on their members' behalf, but have extended their remits to cover conferences and courses addressing the perennial issues confronting families, such as succession planning and transition to the next generation. Private banks which have a significant client base of wealthy families also have staff with the experience and knowledge to advise on these areas.

The rising economic clout of family businesses and the wealth of their owners have altered the picture. Every corporate advisor of significance, such as the major accountancy firms, has a department dedicated to the family business: we have featured some of their reports and surveys already. They have always had an interest, of course, as a proportion of their client base has been family-controlled enterprises. But two important changes have happened in recent years: the scale of their investment in this area has rapidly increased as the economic value of this line of business has grown, and they have broadened their offer to address the supposedly "soft" issues of personal relationships inherent in family businesses, which are often the hardest to resolve. To this end, they have beefed up their consultancy arms either through recruiting and developing talent or through acquisition. For example, Deloitte's UK business acquired leading family consultants Peter Leach & Partners[22] in October 2014 as their way of expanding into this sector.

Leach, who is now again independent, is widely considered to be the founding father of family business consulting[23] in the UK. He created the Stoy Hayward Centre for Family Business [now incorporated into BDO] and has published widely in the field. He explains his approach in *Family Enterprises: The Essentials*:

> This is not consulting in the traditional sense of client-visiting, fact-gathering and report-writing. Family business advising and consulting offers families expert facilitation, trust-building, support and guidance services that support family members, helping them to arrive at their own solutions and their own consensus as to the best way forward.[24]

Early in the book, Leach describes how much of his thinking was influenced by learning from the US pioneers in the field of family business consulting: like so much else in the consulting industry, American practitioners led the way. Leach, in turn, has made his own contribution, not just through his own consulting practice and books, but by mentoring the rising generation of practitioners in the field. It is a discipline that, for obvious reasons, requires immense powers of diplomacy and empathy, coupled with knowing the right time to address what might well amount to herds of elephants in the room.

It is also a business that demands utmost discretion. No family wants their dirty laundry aired in public. Generally speaking, the services of family business consultants have been called in historically when a family business has reached a critical juncture, crisis even, such as a situation in which there is no existing mechanism for resolving disagreements, managing governance, or enabling succession. A frequent cause of friction lies in conversations that zig-zag across the boundaries of running the business, share ownership and membership in the family. All too often, the woman who occupies the position of matriarch is at the centre of the storm, burdened with the role of CEO: Chief Emotional

Officer, not a formal appointment but a highly demanding one, caught between the conflicting demands of different generations.

Each family situation is unique, but the issues are nearly always the generic ones we have already referred to. They are made more intractable by divorce, remarriage and the growth of the family over the generations. In the second generation, the family business is commonly defined as a "sibling partnership," assuming there is more than one child to take over the management/ownership of the enterprise. From the third generation onwards, it is commonly described as a "cousin consortium," and it is at this point that the problems tend to intensify and the services of the consultant are required. The more people there are, the more points of view there are likely to be. At the root of the problem in most cases is that messy overlap between the family, the running of the business and the questions around ownership. For that reason, family business consultants commonly operate with the Three-Circle Model as their primary diagnostic tool.

Sometimes It's Best to Go Your Separate Ways ...

In July 2021, one of Germany's largest family-controlled food and beverage companies announced it was splitting in two. At the time, the Oetker Group had sales of US$4.3 billion, and some 17,000 employees in 400 subsidiaries across Europe, the Americas, Asia, Africa, and Australia. In Europe, it is best known for its Dr Oetker-branded baking powder and frozen pizza products, but the group was active in the bakeries, chemicals, hotels, wine, transport, and finance sectors as well.

The company was founded by chemist August Oetker in 1891 to manufacture baking powder. It expanded steadily by organic growth and acquisition, both in Germany and overseas. From 1944, the business was led by August's grandson, Rudolf-August, who grew the company rapidly, turning it into one of the country's most admired Mittelstand firms. The company's associations with the deposed Nazi regime were conveniently swept under the carpet. By all accounts, Rudolph-August was a demanding, patriarchal figure, renowned for his frugality. He married three times, thus creating different branches of descendants, all with shares in the family firm.

By the second decade of the 21st century, the senior management and ownership of the company were largely in the hands of the fifth generation, which in practice meant eight heirs of Rudolf-August, an assortment of siblings, half-siblings, and cousins. The Oetker Group fitted the description of a cousin consortium, with the multiple differences of opinion and temperament that implies. Family disagreements, however, were kept largely within the family.

When the division of the business was made public, it caught public opinion by surprise. From the press releases issued, it was apparent that the five heirs to Rudolf-August from his first and second marriages had combined to take control of the Group's main food business, Dr Oetker, along with Coppenrath & Wiese [bakery], Radeberger Gruppe [beverages], and Flaschenpost [beverage delivery], plus assets in transport and hotels. The other three heirs took over the remaining assets in the form of a food ingredients company, a sparkling wine business, a chemical firm, a finance enterprise, and hotels in Paris and Venice. Their holding company was to be known as Geschwister Oetker Beteiligungen. That too remains a privately held concern, under the control of Ferdinand and Alfred Oetker.

There is no public account of the disputes which must have led up to the split. Officially, the division of the Group is ascribed to differences over the firm's strategic direction. *Just Food* newsletter reported that a separation agreement – presumably legally binding – was due to appear later the same year.

Sources: www.oetker.com/about-us/our-history; www.dw.com/en/another-german-company-reveals-its-nazi-past/a-17174930; *Just Food, 23 July 2021.*

The family consultant typically starts an engagement with multiple one-to-one conversations to ascertain the views and concerns of family members. Based on what they have learned, the consultant will then go on to facilitate a series of conversations between family members and generations who may well have lost the art of communicating successfully with their siblings, cousins, parents and children. The conversations are designed to enable the various individuals to understand each other's points of view in a way which establishes common ground and takes much of the heat out of what may seem an intractable set of impasses. The aim, as Leach describes above, is to enable the family to work through the issues themselves and to "own" the agreed outcomes and solutions themselves. Part of the facilitator's skill is to seed the discussion with concepts from his or her own toolbox of structures and processes that provide clarity and direction, so that the right conversations happen in the right place at the right time.

One of the starting points is to separate the governance of the firm from the management of the family, and to formalise the relationship between the two.

Any family will have its own rituals and customs. Few of them ever attempt to write these down or uncover the values and beliefs which unconsciously underpin them. A *Family Constitution* attempts to do exactly that, to create in detail a document that defines why the family does what it does, what it is trying to achieve, and the values by which its members should live their lives. If this sounds trite, superficial, or a statement of the obvious, it rarely is. It can take a large family a good three years to create an agreed constitution which all can buy into: it has to cover the resolution of current disputes, how foreseeable divergences of opinion can be resolved, bring to the surface hitherto unspoken assumptions, and in many cases set "penalties" for transgressive behaviour. A good constitution will also lay out the forums for discussion that allow everyone's voices to be heard. These would typically include a *Family Council*, attended by all members, a *Family Business Forum*, attended by those members who work in the business, and a *Non-Business Family Forum*, where spouses and others who do not work in the firm can express their opinions. These latter two forums feed into the *Family Council*, so all members are kept informed of what is being discussed and what the outcomes are of those discussions. Such a system has another big advantage: these two forums, which separate those who work in the business from those who don't, are a mechanism for airing and resolving disagreements *before* they can fester and enable those who attend them to speak with one voice. In the early days of setting these arrangements up, the consultant may well be asked to act as Chair[person] or moderator.

The Family Enterprise Consultant

Alex Sharpe is a co-founder and principal of Kinestra Partners, a leading London-based family enterprise consultancy. She has worked in this field for some 15 years and is a chartered accountant as well as the holder of a Master's in Organisational and Social Psychology from the London School of Economics.

"If I could sum up this role in a nutshell, it's about combining profit with purpose. It's a blend of the deeply personal and the commercial. To be effective, one must understand the business and ownership issues that families face, as well as be comfortable navigating the often-tricky interpersonal dynamics. A single conversation can cut across numerous areas that concern both the business and the family. Working with family businesses is complex and challenging, but also extremely rewarding."

Alex's work tends to focus on inter-generational transition, and the starting point of every engagement is to pose the question "what would success look like for the next phase?" The answer is unique to each family, and Alex regards her job as opening her clients' eyes to the universe of possible solutions. Families contact Kinestra for multiple reasons, but one of the most frequent is a family wishing to consider how to move forward after the death of a patriarch or matriarch, which throws many things into question. "Typically, it will be some time, say a couple of years, after a parent has deceased, that we will be asked to help. The family needs time to grieve and then to take stock of the new circumstances. Alternatively, a catalyst might be the next generation becoming involved and the resultant need to integrate them successfully. Another reason could be that there are communication issues between family members, which we are asked to help resolve. Sometimes my work involves taking on family/corporate governance roles – I act as Chair of a number of Family Councils, either mentoring the family to self-sufficiency or as a permanent member of the team."

There will normally be a family member who "sponsors" the engagement, but Alex makes it clear from the outset that her client is the family as a whole. "Our aim is always to aid the family in determining what is best for them. While every situation is unique, there are some common features in the consultancy process. There will be a phase of discovery and diagnosis, in the form of multiple conversations, followed by sensitive feedback of what we have found that flushes out where there is consensus and where there is further work to be done. Then there follows a series of facilitated discussions with different groups as we get to a resolution and an agreed way forward. We use the joint development of documentation with the family as a shared agenda and to keep everyone on track."

Kinestra's clientele is broadly speaking divided 50/50 between UK and overseas families. However, Alex is wary of bringing cultural or other assumptions to the table. "It's dangerous to approach an engagement by categorising a family enterprise as this or that in advance, and pre-judging the solution. Yes, we have a toolbox of structures and processes, but no one size fits all. Some families are looking to create legacy and longevity, while for some it may not actually be in the best interests of the rising generation to continue owning the family business if, for example, their motive is primarily to honour the memory of the founder. Sometimes an outright sale or division of assets might be a happier outcome all round, and our role is to help families to have these conversations."

In the time that she has worked in family business consultancy, Alex has noticed a change in her clients' attitudes, perhaps because of a better awareness of the issues. "When I started we were seen to a large extent as people who could help solve a problem. Now the starting point is much more 'can you help us be the best that we can be?' From my point of view, that's a very positive development."

Finally, Alex is keen to stress that she and her colleagues are not dispute mediators. "There are others who do that job. We assist families in defining their purpose and collectively creating the future that they want for themselves."

Source: In conversation with the author. Alex was also in partnership with Peter Leach when Peter Leach & Partners LLP was sold to Deloitte, where she became Head of Family Enterprise Consulting for the UK.

It might sound like the norms of corporate culture – bureaucracy and decision by committee – are being imposed on an independent business that thrives on agility and an entrepreneurial spirit. So there is a balance to be struck, and possibly a certain amount of experimentation to see what works. But experience and the overwhelming evidence from history suggest that this kind of approach is a far better means of preserving family unity. No one size fits all: if the family has a strong belief in philanthropy, for instance, this can also be accommodated through a specific forum, whose wishes can equally be fed into the Family Council. It is also inevitable that, as the family *business* grows through multiple generations, it has no choice but to formalise many of its processes and systems. Good governance in family relations bleeds into good corporate governance. No longer are big decisions invariably taken by the person with the loudest voice. As a final point, those who work inside the family business do not necessarily have a monopoly on wisdom or good ideas. This kind of process broadens the field of contribution.

Other Advisors

The preceding sections have outlined the roles played by the most commonly used advisors to UHNW families. There are others, usually called on when a family member has a specific interest, such as collecting art or classic cars. Such people are frequently found through the existing network of friends and advisors which the family has created over the years – and which curator, after all, would have declined to work with JP Getty and his heirs to populate the museum that bears his name in Los Angeles, or which architect would have passed up the opportunity to design and build it?[25]

In Conclusion

- Today's UHNW family enjoys an extensive eco-system of support services. Some of those services exist to maintain and enhance the assets possessed by the family, while others are there to support the family in a private capacity. Yet others, such as business schools and information providers, such as websites and magazines, straddle both areas. This circle of trusted providers can be envisaged very much like the courts that surrounded royalty and the more powerful aristocratic families of the Middle Ages and the Renaissance.
- That circle expands over time, as generations multiply and family wealth, whether in the form primarily of a business entity or as a diverse portfolio of assets, grows incrementally [through compounding interest] or exponentially [through one-off business deals, such as the purchase and sale of football clubs]. The basis of that circle is first and foremost trust.
- A growing proportion of that family wealth, probably the majority, is managed by family offices, either single or multi-family. These entities not only advise on the management of the family's wealth, but also oversee the investment and the structuring of the vehicles, such as trusts, to control it. Their numbers are expanding rapidly, powered in large part by the rise in family wealth in regions such as the Middle East and Asia-Pacific. The remit of family offices has also broadened to embrace areas of interest to family members, such as philanthropy.
- Family Offices are themselves very diverse, subject to the cultures in which they operate and the backgrounds of the families they serve. In North America, the relationship is essentially a professional one. Elsewhere, notably in Europe and the Middle East, the ties tend to be more personal, and other values such as status, branding and prestige come into play.
- To maintain the modern UHNW family's lifestyle, a huge range of service providers has grown up. The advisory circle also tends to expand as family wealth grows and family members increase. Specialist advisors support parents and children from pregnancy through early years, primary, secondary and even tertiary education. Concierge services and private members clubs for the newly enriched fulfil the roles historically played by the country houses and household staff enjoyed by aristocratic families. The purchase of these services is as required, and the relationship is essentially a transactional one.
- The *lingua franca* of today's globally mobile UHNW family is English, and that is reflected in the international prevalence of US and British-based schools modelled on those countries' traditions. Again, in areas like the Middle East and Asia-Pacific, branding and heritage play an important role in parental choice.

- A new breed of consultant has emerged to meet the needs of multi-generational families and the assets they control, which grow more complex over the years. Their role is to bring clarity over the differences between ownership, management and family roles and to help their clients design the structures and processes that enable everyone's voice to be heard and which minimise conflict.

* * *

In Chapter 4, we take a look into the future: what does it hold for the wealthy family business of tomorrow, and how will the generations that stand to inherit enormous fortunes consume and steward their legacies?

Notes

1 2023 Edelman Trust Barometer Global Final Report, p. 47.
2 13 August 2024.
3 See later in this chapter for the answer.
4 Explained later in this chapter.
5 It is actually the Wharton School of the University of Pennsylvania, founded in 1881.
6 At the end of 2024 Rupert lost the battle and one can only imagine the state of relations within the family. The decision was then reversed on appeal.
7 This section has greatly benefited from discussion with Alexander Rupert von der Vellen.
8 www.hbs.edu/faculty/Pages/item.aspx?num=47167#:~:text=Abstract,American%20business%20and%20economic%20history. Elon Musk may well overtake Rockefeller.
9 Posted on LinkedIn, 24 March 2024.
10 Reported in Wealth Briefing, 1 March 2024.
11 Essentially those born in the last two decades of the 20th century.
12 Phoenix, 1993, second edition.
13 The College first accepted a male trainee nanny in 1999. The number of men applying still remains very small.
14 Founded in Dubai in 1961, to educate the children of expatriates working in the oil industry.
15 It does not always work out. Malvern College's partnership venture in Leysin, Switzerland, closed in 2022 within a short time of opening.
16 Vikram Mathur, Rupa Publications Private Ltd.
17 https://jobs.tutors.international
18 Trapeze Publications.
19 Mercury Homesearch website.
20 One Irish developer was also involved.
21 See www.agreus.com

22 Leach assumed the role of Global Head of Family Enterprising.
23 Nominated by Family Capital as one of the Top 100 Family Influencers.
24 Profile Books, 2016.
25 Under the umbrella of the Getty Centre, the museum is now housed on two campuses: after its patron's death, those administering the collection were embroiled for years in accusations of illegal trafficking in antiquities.

Further Reading

Stewardship: Twelve Families and the Art of Lasting Wealth, Von der Wellen, Alexander, self-published, available via Amazon.

Family Enterprises: The Essentials, Leach, Peter, 2016, Profile Books, London.

The Family Business Book: A Roadmap for Entrepreneurial Families to Prosper Across Generations, De Massis, Alfredo and Rondi, Emmanuela, 2024, FT Publishing International, London.

4
The Tsunami of Wealth: More Money than the World Has Ever Seen

Introduction

The next two decades will be a better time than ever before to be in the asset management business. The wave of inherited money to be transferred between the generations will be almost incomprehensibly enormous. To describe it as a tsunami is to understate the magnitude. Drawing from data collected by wealth management specialists Cerulli Associates, the *Financial Times* of 27 December 2024 reported that over US$100 trillion of assets held in the United States alone will be inherited over the next 25 years from parents and grandparents by the rising generation of Americans. In their *High-Net-Worth and Ultra-High-Net-Worth Report*, Cerulli projects that US$105 trillion will flow to US heirs, over 50% of this from the 2% of residents who collectively comprise the high-net-worth [HNW] and ultra-high-net-worth [UHNW] population [jointly defined as households with investible assets over US$5 million]. The same article reported that *Vanguard*, another wealth management company, predicted that by 2030 US$18 trillion would be transferred between generations worldwide. That equates to the best part of US$4 trillion annually on average, across the globe.

What will the eventual resting place be for these assets, and who will be the beneficiaries of this phenomenon? These are two of the primary questions this chapter of the book will attempt to answer, along with describing the challenges and opportunities created by a trend that will confront governments across the world.

The *second* of these questions, concerning who will benefit, is perhaps the least controversial to answer. Past patterns of behaviour and basic demographic data provide the foundation for some solid assumptions. In addition to family recipients, Cerulli conjectures that a considerable sum, US$18 trillion, will pass to charities. [For context, for the year 2023–2024 London-based consultancy

DOI: 10.4324/9781003685487-5

Legacy Futures put the income of UK charities deriving from wills at £4.1 billion: most of this was from wealthy donors, the 9% who accounted for nearly 60% of the giving.[1]]

This tallies both with the American tradition of philanthropy and the stated aim of the super-rich, such as Bill Gates and Warren Buffett, that the bulk of their personal fortunes will pass to not-for-profit foundations, not to their children.[2] In 2010, Gates and Buffett founded the *Giving Pledge*, a campaign to persuade the rich to donate a minimum of half their wealth to charitable causes.[3] Both individuals and families were in their sights. Within months, the initiative had garnered some 40 signatories, all American, with a combined wealth of US$125 billion. Some of these donations are to be distributed during the donors' lifetimes, and some on their decease. In 2014, the campaign leaders created a "Nextgen" affiliate, specifically to meet the needs of the living descendants of pledgers, who express an interest in learning more about philanthropy to create their own initiatives. In early 2025, the campaign website reported that over 240 signatories from 30 different countries had made their pledges. Giving Pledge does not disclose the wealth of those who sign up, but in 2018 a report issued by Wealth-X[4] estimated the combined net worth of signatories at US$600 billion. Presumably, this sum is even greater by now.

The Cerulli report also estimates that 90% or so of this inherited wealth will derive from the generation dubbed Baby Boomers, that is to say those born between 1946 and 1964. [Born in 1957, I am pretty much in the middle years of this cohort.] The oldest of this generation are now approaching their 80s, and the youngest are just entering their 60s. As men in general have a lower life expectancy than women, in the first instance much of this wealth will pass horizontally to widows and partners who outlive the deceased, before reaching the next generation. Wealthy Boomer women, as we shall see, tend to take a serious interest in philanthropic and charitable causes.

The *first* of these questions, the eventual destination of the inherited assets, is less straightforward to answer. As I have argued, the basis of much wealth enjoyed by today's rich families ultimately derives from the businesses founded by visionary entrepreneurs and passed on through the generations. Over time, a proportion of that asset-based wealth may well have been turned into cash through a public listing – like that of Walmart, the retailer controlled by the Walton family – or the family business may remain a purely private enterprise, like the Louis Dreyfus Company, the mighty multinational food and commodities concern. The next-generation heirs to these firms will have to decide whether they wish to continue as family-controlled and managed entities or whether the family members will cash out in favour of transforming themselves into a business family, where ownership of a single corporation no longer forms the major part of their assets. That decision is not always solely in the hands of family members. Markets change, the unexpected can overturn the best-laid plans, and occasionally offers arise that are simply too good to refuse. It is also unknowable whether the formula for the longevity of a family business, which I outlined earlier in this book, will continue to apply indefinitely.

However, *the near-term future of the eco-system* which supports the HNW and UHNW families in the coming years looks unquestionably bright. I have already mentioned the growth in the wealth management industry, which shows no sign of slowing. Family offices will compete for the best talent, and private banks will flourish. Other providers of upscale goods and services can expect to do brisk business: Rolls-Royce Cars certainly seems to share the optimistic belief in a steady flow of rich buyers. On 9 January 2025, the company announced it would be investing £300 million in its Goodwood plant in Sussex, to support future expansion. Most of the cars produced will undoubtedly go for export. In November the previous year, Bentley promoted the creation of the "Bentley Mews," the repurposing of the old CEO's country house close to the Crewe factory, a space in which buyers can immerse themselves in the marque's heritage and commission their new vehicle to their own specification. It is true that some luxury goods brands have recently reported a slowdown: there is after all a limit to the number of £3,000 handbags that one person can reasonably purchase, and major cities like London and New York have experienced a rise in the brazen theft of upmarket accessories like branded bags and watches that are openly visible on the street. That said, the growing vogue for discreet luxury provides ample opportunity for new product development.[5]

Business schools and other providers of education for the next generation of wealthy family members will benefit. In my final years of teaching in a UK business school, I was struck by the number of places taken on Master's programmes by this cohort: as many as half the students on these courses were next-generation members of family businesses, preparing themselves to assume stewardship at some point of the legacy handed to them. The demand for high-quality childcare also continues. Around the start of 2025, the UK press carried numerous reports of wealthy Democrat-voting families fleeing the US to London in advance of Donald Trump assuming the Presidency.[6] Their younger children will need nannies and nursery care, and their older children schooling. Parents will, in many cases, need a hand to help them navigate the quirks of living in Britain, where a crib is a cot, a stroller is a pushchair, and public schools signify private education. The transition to a new life will be eased by the international character of so many upscale brands with which the rich are already familiar, including the members' clubs and concierge services that have proliferated in the last two decades.

Governments, however, are torn by conflicting priorities. On the one hand, Western European demographics point to a continuing need for younger immigrants to perform the healthcare and other jobs that domestic populations are unable or unwilling to undertake. On the other hand, these countries' electorates are concerned about the unintended consequences of mass immigration and the seeming inability of their governments to control it. A clear resolution of this tension has yet to emerge. Since the financial crash of 2007/2008, economic growth in Western European economies has been sluggish by comparison with the US, Asia-Pacific, and the Middle East. Southern Europe, in particular Spain, Italy and Portugal, as part of the solution, has embarked on a drive to attract wealthy retirees and younger entrepreneurs through tax breaks and other incentives. Sunshine, attractive cities, nice beaches and a relaxed lifestyle certainly help. At the same time, locals complain that they are being priced out of the housing market [Spain, like the UK, seems to have fallen badly short in building new housing], while visitor hotspots like Barcelona and Venice argue that they are overwhelmed by mass tourism and are seeking to cap the numbers by daily charges. In a seeming about-turn, at the start of 2025 the Spanish government announced plans to impose property taxes of 100% on non-EU property purchasers,[7] which is bad news for the British. Governments of all colours have multiple constituencies to placate, which does not always produce internally consistent policies. Britain, meanwhile, has seen a net exodus of the wealthy, both UK nationals and foreign residents, in reaction to recent measures imposed or proposed by the Labour administration. Their taxes – not merely income, but consumption, council/property, and sales taxes – will be paid elsewhere.[8]

The truth is that many of those who run nation-states seem reluctant or unable to come to terms with the new age of global mobility for the wealthy.

Generations Apart

As any parent knows, the rising generation tends to want to do things differently from those who raised them. It's true of music, art, fashion, food, architecture, and much else to do with culture. It also seems to be the case with money and how you spend and invest it. There is a growing band of consultancies and market research agencies specialising in profiling the tastes, priorities, and aspirations of the different generations, which seem to change at a bewildering pace. Even the nomenclature is puzzling to the layman. The term "[Baby] Boomers," as I've used above, is widely understood, and the age profile defining the cohort is generally accepted as designating those born in the 20 years after the Second World War: Boomers, because that period saw a steady rise in the birth-rate, perhaps nature's way of repopulating the planet after the

Table 4.1 **Generational table**

Generation	*Age cohort*	*Historical events**	*Prime concerns*	*Stereotyped as*	*Communicate mainly by*
Boomers	Born between 1946 and 1964	• Cold War • Space Race • Nuclear Proliferation • Retreat from Empire	Security and stability	Pragmatic and hard-nosed conservative [small c]	Telephone and text/email
Gen X	Born between 1965 and 1981	• End of Cold War • Cheap travel • Early computers	Work–life balance	Flexible and independent	Email and social media: e.g. LinkedIn, Facebook
Gen Y/ Millennials	Born between 1982 and mid 1990s	• Collapse of Soviet Union • Mass migrations • Rise of China, India, and ME • Internet dominates	Causes and activism Employee rights	Prone to teamwork, overqualified, lacking maturity	Social media: e.g. WhatsApp, Instagram
Gen Z	Born between 1997 and 2012	• Global warming • Arab Spring • Cloud computing • COVID-19	Job stability Job mobility	Multitasking Short attention spans Addicted to social networks	Social media: e.g. TikTok, WhatsApp
Generation Alpha	Born between 2010 and 2024	To come	To come	Digital Natives	?

Table created by the author. Primary sources: Iberdrola Talent Report, Modern Affluence/Future Laboratory Summit Report. * As impacting on later teenage years and adulthood loss of so many lives. This demographic bump, plus the falling birth rates seen throughout the West largely explain today's increasing strain on healthcare for the elderly. However, the terms "Millennials" and "Gen Y" are used interchangeably, and refer to the same cohort born between the early 1980s and the mid 1990s. In the Table above, I have set out these classifications, for my own benefit as much as anything, so there is clarity over what we are talking about. The Table basically combines findings from two organisations that have made their research into the generations publicly available. Spanish-based *Iberdrola* is the second-largest energy business in the UK, owning both Scottish Power and Electricity North West, and has a major presence in renewables, specifically wind power: it claims to be the only UK utility business that generates 100% of its electricity from renewable sources. This aligns with the concerns of more recent generations and accounts for their consumer market research focus. The *Modern Affluence Exchange* is a London-based consultancy that specifically examines and reports on the priorities and attitudes of those inheritors of significant family wealth, based on research conducted by *The Future Laboratory*.

The Table delineates for each generation the chief historical events that have shaped their development while growing up, what seem to be their prime concerns, how they are stereotypically perceived by the rest of us, and their communication preferences. For completeness – and so you can understand the reference – I have added the latest cohort to feature in the media, Generation Alpha [commentators resort to the Greek alphabet when they run out of Latin letters], though most of these have yet to hit puberty and so have still to play their part in this story.

Many of the people reading this book – perhaps the majority – will be *Boomers*. We grew up in a bipolar world, our formative years spent witnessing the space race, the proliferation of nuclear weapons, and the retreat from empire of the Western European powers. There were heroes and villains, the labels subject to which side of the Berlin Wall you lived. The Cold War and, for the older Boomers, the reconstruction of Europe after the Second World War, shaped those who lived in the West. Not surprisingly, security and stability are major concerns, and we tend to be conservative with a small c. We are notoriously reluctant to embrace new information technology, and we stick with what we know [though I have highly IT-literate friends in their 70s who buck the trend]. These traits are reflected in our attitudes towards money, and a preference for investment in tangible things like property and stocks – at least you have proof of value in the form of a share certificate – and works of art, fine wines and spirits if you have sufficient surplus income. Boomers are correspondingly suspicious of "alternative assets" such as cryptocurrencies and non-fungible tokens [we'll come to these later]. There is a strong case for arguing that Boomers' preferences are the major factor behind the price inflation of assets like property, where they park the wealth they have accumulated over their lifetimes. Apart from blips such as the oil crisis of the early 1970s, Boomers have lived their lives through a period of constant economic growth, making this the wealthiest generation in human history; by some estimates, more than 30 times richer than Generation Z.[9]

Generation X, the cohort born over the next 15 years or so [1965–1981], has grown up witnessing the end of the Cold War, the ability to travel cheaply and relatively often, and the dawn of the personal computer age [Microsoft and Apple were founded in 1975 and 1976, respectively]. For this generation, the weight of a bipolar world was largely lifted from their shoulders. In 1989, the US historian Francis Fukuyama published his influential article "The End of History" in the journal *The National Interest* and reached a much wider audience three years later with his book *The End of History and the Last Man*, which posited the idea that the West and Western values had emerged in triumph. Communism was effectively over, and a progressive era of liberal democracy was now the new global norm. "The peace dividend" meant that spending on warfare could be diverted increasingly to welfare: the UK's current defence spending, which as a percentage of GDP is about a quarter of what it was in the 1950s, is a prime example. Generation X also benefited from economies with healthy rates of growth and were able to spend their disposable incomes on consuming the cheap travel created by the emerging business models of South West Airlines, EasyJet, Ryanair and the like. This cohort also seems less absorbed by work and more concerned with a better balance between work and life, while being seen at the same time as flexible and independent. It is perhaps no coincidence that entrepreneurship begins to emerge in this period as an alternative career path. Those with money to invest are prone to diversifying from traditional asset classes and into innovation such as cryptocurrencies. According to The Modern Affluence Exchange, the investment and purchasing preferences of wealthy members of this cohort are also strongly influenced by the ethical and socially responsible credentials of the brands and companies they favour.

Next in line, *Generation Y* or *Millennials*, are those born in the two decades leading up to the year 2000, between 1982 and the mid 1990s. For this cohort, the Soviet Union has either collapsed or is old history. Eastern Europe is being transformed. Some countries enjoy relative peace and prosperity, knocking on the door of the European Union. Others, notably the Balkan states, are embroiled in the centuries-old feuds and vendettas that had formerly simmered beneath the lid of communist dictatorship, and are now unleashed. Millions of more fortunate Eastern Europeans are taking advantage of their new freedoms to live and work in the West – and millions of young Westerners are taking advantage of the cheap flights offered by the emerging low-cost airlines to explore the charms of Tallinn, Prague, and Budapest. In the early 1990s, I found myself for the first time in Warsaw on business and witnessed at first-hand a society in rapid transition, the young enthusiastic in their embrace of Western brands and media while their elders were seeking to adjust to both the opportunities and downsides of free enterprise. Mass migration in Europe from East to West[10] was on a scale not seen since the latter days of the Roman Empire. In Britain, where restrictions on newcomers imposed by other Western members of the EU were not copied by the Blair government, immigration was in the hundreds of thousands, if not millions. This, combined with frequent travel to continental Europe, created in Generation Y a mindset more receptive to the notion of multiculturalism. At the same time, the Middle East, China and India were accounting for an ever-growing share of world economic activity: the countries of the Arabian peninsula were recording huge annual trade surpluses, China overtook the US in share of world trade in the mid-2010s, and between 2000 and 2024 India tripled its share of world trade.[11] The opening of this cohort's eyes to global possibilities was accelerated, of course, by the growing importance in everyday life of the internet. What was a novelty for Boomers was just part of business as usual for Generation Y and had profound changes on what they consumed, read and watched.

Lastly[12] comes *Generation Z*, the cohort defined as those born between 1997 and 2012: the generation that has either recently entered the workforce/seeking work, or is still in education. Environmental concerns are a major preoccupation for this generation, if only because they are the people who will be living with the consequences if the scientific consensus about global warming proves correct, and who will be those having to deal with it. Many have also lived through the Arab Spring that commenced in 2010, that short-lived era when it was hoped that the politics of much of North Africa and the Middle East would be transformed along Fukuyama lines, only to witness the present-day turmoil that pervades a great part of the region. The nirvana of liberal democracy everywhere remains elusive. Technology has embedded itself in every aspect of Generation Z's lives: they are notoriously reliant on their smartphones from sunrise to sunset, and in the eyes of the older generation, live their lives online at least as much as in real life. Across the world, their education was seriously disrupted by Covid. The career opportunities which their predecessors took for granted are no longer available: they do not expect a lifetime's employment with one employer. Many live from one short-term contract to the next. Housing costs are prohibitive in the major cities to which young people have traditionally flocked, and large numbers have little choice but to live in the parental home. Above all, this is the first generation since the Second World War that, by and large, can expect to be significantly poorer than their predecessors.

However, there are some important qualifications to this picture.

First, this characterisation is a broad-brush approach. It does not apply equally across all countries and all income brackets. Boomers are *on the whole* significantly wealthier than Generation Z, but by no means in every case. Not all members of Generation Z are created equal, either. There is a startling disparity between the US and the UK. In the States, those born in this cohort have lived through an average annual growth rate in the economy of 2.5%. Until 2010, the UK more or less kept up with the US [the LSE cites a figure of 2.2%[13]], but from then on the equivalent figure has been dismal, struggling to hit 1%.[14] In the *Financial Times* on 24 January 2025, John Burn-Murdoch reported that "Americans born in 1995 are enjoying even more upward mobility relative to their parents than those born in 1965." Burn-Murdoch speculates that the growing wealth of this cohort may well widen social divisions within America, and may also partly explain Donald Trump's election success: winners, notably younger female voters, flocked towards someone who promised them more of the same.

Second, these blanket descriptions conceal social trends which run in a counter-direction. I have mentioned the rise in entrepreneurship, which becomes noticeable with the Millennials, or Generation X. In the immediate post-war period, anyone who could tended to embrace the security of working for a large organisation, and in all likelihood stayed with that employer for a lifetime's employment. While working for yourself always had status in the US, it was typically less well-regarded in Europe and particularly so in Britain. That changed, in large part because big organisations that had once seemed to be an immutable part of the landscape, like the chemicals giant ICI and motor manufacturers British Motor Corporation [later British Leyland], fragmented or simply disappeared. It was true also in the US: in the technology sector alone, once-dominant businesses like Burroughs, Honeywell and the much-diminished IBM are no longer household names. An ever-growing number of people created their own employment, and pioneer Boomer role models such as Bill Gates, Steve Jobs, James Dyson, and Richard Branson have inspired their peers and the generations that followed. In a word, entrepreneurship became sexy – and that spilt over into perceptions of family business. These weren't mere mom-and-pop shops, but serious businesses offering great careers for both family members and others.

Third, averages across large populations tend to mislead. The inheritors of significant family wealth are a breed apart, not typical of the average Generation Z. They have enjoyed access to elite education and all the trappings of a global, mobile lifestyle. They have been largely cushioned from the effects of political upheavals and social turmoil, and rarely need to raise a mortgage to acquire a place to live. On the other hand, these fortunate few have witnessed the same historical events and been shaped by the same cultural forces as their less well-off peers. If you have no pressing need to make your way in the world and the time and money to indulge your tastes and curiosity, you are well-placed to lead the way in adopting emerging art forms and new technologies. In *The Great Wealth Transfer,*[15] a report accompanying The Modern Affluence Summit of 2023, The Modern Affluence Exchange identifies the consumption trends and preferences of what they describe as the 0.1% of the global population: that tiny fraction nevertheless equals around 8 million people, composed mainly of Generations Y and Z. Their attitudes and behaviour are further explored in the pages that follow.

The report also predicts that Generations Y and Z in the US alone will inherit a staggering £42 trillion [US$53 trillion, €49 trillion, at 2023 exchange rates] by 2045. What will they do with it? As noted above, an awful lot – the report puts the figure at £9.4 trillion – will flow into charitable causes. In many cases, the inheriting generation will devote most, if not all, of their "working life" to supervising the philanthropic foundations which they or their parents have established. Philanthropy, yes, but not necessarily as we have known it in the past.

Philanthropy in Transition

In the Gates Foundation, the Gates family has created in two decades the world's third largest[16] charitable entity ranked by value of endowments: as at the end of 2023, these were valued at US$75.2 billion. Its stated goals are to enhance healthcare and reduce extreme poverty across the world, and to expand educational opportunities and access to information technology in the United States. [The aims of the Giving Pledge, described earlier, cover these fields as well, but include initiatives to combat or alleviate the effects of climate change, disaster relief and the promotion of arts and culture]. The Gates Foundation undertakes numerous initiatives off its own bat, such as the funding of around 100 graduate students annually at the University of Cambridge, partners with the research programmes of other institutions, and contributes to the work of agencies such as the World Health Organisation [WHO], a UN body. The driving forces, Bill and Melinda, are, of course, of the Boomer generation.

The Foundation is the result of merging Bill and Melinda's own Foundation with that of Bill's father, William H Gates II [Bill is formally William H Gates III]. When the Gates couple divorced in 2021, Bill took the role of sole Chairman. It makes an interesting and important example to study, not just because of Gates' high profile, but because it forms a template for the direction in which much family philanthropy has been going for the last two decades: as a movement with charitable aims, but managed in a highly business-like way. This approach has been termed venture philanthropy. To this end, the Gates organisation is split into two parts: the Foundation, which chooses where to spend the money generated by the endowment, and a Trust, managed by a board, which oversees the investment portfolio of the endowment. Both the Foundation and the Trust employ experienced professionals, and Bill Gates serves on the Board of Trustees. In essence, the Foundation is managed in a manner that is indistinguishable from a modern corporation, in which the founder plays a very considerable part: in 2008, Gates stepped out of his operational role at Microsoft to devote more of his energies to the Foundation.

Information about the next generation of the Gates family is notoriously difficult to find. The family guard their privacy. The eldest, Jennifer, who is a qualified doctor, was born in 1996, placing her at the tail end of Generation Y: her two male siblings are of Generation Z. From what is in the public domain it appears that all three children are engaged in philanthropy of some kind and there is speculation that they will at some point become involved in the Gates Foundation. The clock is ticking, as the Foundation is obliged to disburse all its funding – effectively dissolve itself – within twenty years of Bill Gates' death, to avoid the fate of many charities accused of degenerating into self-perpetuating bureaucracies that provide jobs for their employees and do little to serve the causes for which they were founded.

The Significance of the Female Philanthropist

In 2022, Altrata,[17] a multinational firm specialising in providing market intelligence to suppliers of services to the ultra-rich,[18] such as private banks and consultancies, produced the *World Ultra Wealth Report*. The landscape it surveyed was affected by recent events, notably Russia's invasion of Ukraine and the COVID-19-epidemic, and the Report found that the wealth of this population was adversely impacted. The number of individuals who met Altrata's wealth threshold of US$30 million dropped by 6%, and the average value of assets owned by those who still qualified as UHNW individuals reduced. The very rich were on the whole marginally less rich. However, much of the Report concerned itself with longer-term trends in the composition of the ultra-rich population, and the marked growth in the number of wealthy women. Their numbers still accounted for only 11% of the UHNW population, but were on the rise. In a quarter of cases, female wealth was inherited, not self-made, [the comparable figure for men is less than 5%], and they were more inclined than their male counterparts to concern themselves with philanthropy.

This should not come as much of a surprise. As already discussed, women of means were behind much of the momentum driving the philanthropy of the Victorian period. In the 20th century the United States socialite Doris Duke, known as "the richest girl in the world," inherited a vast fortune from her father, the major shareholder in American Tobacco, and spent a great part of her life – and wealth – on philanthropic causes, notably medical research, the restoration of historic Newport, Rhode Island, and promoting black welfare and education in the American south. When she died in 1983, she left a fortune of US$5.3 billion, most of it to charity. The difference today is that the Doris Dukes and Melinda Gateses exist in greater numbers and have the clout to make an even greater impact.

If you drill down further into the Altrata Report, more intriguing findings emerge. Almost one-fifth of UHNW women devote most of their time to philanthropy, and this focus is much more marked among those who have inherited their wealth: over half – 54.4% – report that their time is mostly taken up with charitable organisations [defined as philanthropic and social causes]. The report speculates, quite reasonably, that, freed from the need to earn a living, this segment has the time and perhaps the sense of social obligation to pursue good works. When the genders are compared, the difference in commitment is stark: almost 61% of women list philanthropy as their main pursuit, nearly twice the rating of men at 35.1%. In terms of average age, the gender split is almost identical: the average age of the UHNW women is 63.6 years, and that of men is slightly older, at 64.8 years. This is the Boomer generation, and at the start of this decade, the 2020s, the world's wealth was concentrated firmly in their hands.

The Philanthropy Advisor

After some years of working with UK grant-making organisations, *Emma Beeston* sought a new career challenge. She found it in working with families as a philanthropy advisor. Ten years ago, when Emma first started, the profession was not well-known or understood.

"My initial projects came through referrals from institutions, and my work has continued to grow on the basis of word-of-mouth and referrals from private client advisors. At any one time, I will typically be advising five or six families, some of whom might be people I've worked with over some years. What I like most about this role is the agility of families: if they want to do something, it doesn't have to go through a complex approval and decision-making process. They get on and make it happen!"

Each engagement is to a large degree unique, just as every family is, but there are similarities in the process. Emma will start by listening intensely to all members involved, frequently facilitating conversations, and suggesting the philanthropic options available that might suit the family's wishes. Alongside the family's preferences, Emma conducts research and conversations to ensure that decisions are informed by those most affected by an issue, and by current learning and good practice. After that process of discovery, a plan is created, and then Emma will assist with the implementation.

There is usually some personal connection to the type of project supported. Family members will bring to the table their own skills and experience in deciding where to direct their resources. Typically, her families have between £500,000 and £2 million to give to causes annually. There is a range of activities that resonate with families: mental health, music, youth work, science and education. Geography also plays a part, as there may well be a strong attachment in the family to a place where they wish to help improve people's lives and opportunities – for example, memories of happy family holidays in Cornwall, combined with awareness of local needs, such as homelessness and unemployment.

It's unusual for Emma's clients to create their own foundations from scratch: they increasingly use donor-advised funds. When asked if she works with just a single generation, Emma replies that it can be one or as many as three. In some instances, what emerges from the discovery process is that the philanthropic purpose has drifted as more areas of interest have been added over time. The prime aim of the engagement is to re-focus support to achieve the impact the family is looking for: reducing areas of support from eight disparate categories to two clear priorities, for instance. She cites climate change and young people's participation in the arts.

"What's become clear to me in my work is that for many family members, time is more precious than money. They are very busy people, especially the younger generation; it's the older members who have the time to spare. The senior generation encourages the next generation to step up and see philanthropy as an important educational tool. In turn, the younger generation is respectful of the legacy the family wishes to create. There are always differences of opinion, as you would expect. But these are just as likely to arise between members of the same generation as between the generations. If I can help to create a space for family members to listen to each other and agree on a way forward together, I've done my job."

Source: In conversation with the author.

New Attitudes: The Rise of the Activist

The question then follows: will the generation that inherits significant wealth pursue the same type of philanthropy as its predecessors, or will it go its own way? Taking the Gates Foundation as representative of big, institutional philanthropy, its aims are what might be termed those of "traditional" philanthropy: primarily alleviation of poverty and improvements in healthcare. The enormous quantity of funding allows the Gates Foundation to undertake its initiatives on an even bigger scale than the greatest Victorian philanthropists. As such, they mirror the goals of international non-governmental organisations like the United Nations, and it makes sense that much of the work the Foundation funds marches in lockstep with agencies such as the WHO. Funding better agricultural irrigation systems and improved urban sanitation is not inherently controversial.

Another very strong strand of philanthropy that falls into the category of "traditional" philanthropy is local, community-minded, initiatives which concentrate on the places in which family businesses or founders are located, or where they originate. The town of South Danvers, Massachusetts, even changed its name to Peabody to honour the munificence of its most famous son [see Chapter 1], whose largesse extended to establishing educational institutions in the town of his birth: he might have moved in exalted circles in Europe and the United States, but George Peabody never forgot his roots. As also mentioned earlier, in Britain, the Adnams brewery, where a fourth-generation family member is Chairman of the company, organises an annual beach clean in and around its Southwold location, and supports numerous local charities. Philanthropy takes many forms, and there is no reason to think that this kind of smaller-scale corporate social responsibility will not continue indefinitely.

But reports from organisations like the Modern Affluence Summit suggest a sea-change in the way that affluent members of the generations now coming into serious wealth perceive the uses to which their good fortune[s] be put. For a good many, their money is to be used to promote causes that fall broadly under the heading of social activism: combatting climate change, environmental remediation, gender equality and greater transparency in public and corporate life are all high on their agenda. Some will openly admit that they are motivated by guilt about the wealth they have inherited, or are due to inherit. There is evidence to support the idea that radical causes are largely the preserve of the affluent: a report produced by a combined team of academics from Exeter, Keele, and Aston universities[19] profiled the activists behind Extinction Rebellion as overwhelmingly middle-class and highly educated; the well-heeled backgrounds of Just Stop Oil, a splinter group of Extinction Rebellion, have been the subject of considerable scrutiny in the British press.[20] The Chelsea Flower Show might seem like a bizarre protest venue, but this young generation of activists tends to target the very events, brands, and organisations beloved of their parents and grandparents. The movement's poster girl, Phoebe Plummer, actually grew up in Chelsea and was educated at one of Britain's most expensive private schools.

The Rich People Who Want to Pay More Tax

Patriotic Millionaires was founded in the United States in 2010, as a non-partisan group of wealthy American citizens pressing for the abolition of tax cuts for the rich passed under the Bush administration. Some years later, a British counterpart was established, Patriotic Millionaires UK. Its website currently claims to have "60 plus" members, and the organisation has set itself three central purposes, in pursuit of tackling the crisis [sic] of extreme wealth:

- The rich should pay more, and progressive taxes should rise
- Work should be fairly rewarded, and all stakeholders in society should benefit
- Wealth should not buy or corrupt politics

To these ends, the organisation lobbies politicians, publishes position papers, and allies itself with like-minded causes, such as the Good Ancestor Movement. On Patriotic Millionaires UK's board sit a former City trader, entrepreneurs and environmentalists, a director of a family foundation, and the founder of the B-Corp* movement in Britain, James Perry. Its governing board is chaired by Morris Pearl, a former Managing Director of BlackRock, the world's largest asset manager. The ages and backgrounds of the people actively guiding the organisation align with the Boomer and Generation X age cohorts.

As might be expected, its aims have attracted interest from HNW individuals of more recent generations. An article in the *Sunday Telegraph* on 9 March 2025 featured Paolo Fresia, London-based heir to a family fortune based on vermouth, under the headline "I inherited a windfall – it was a blessing and a curse." Fresia came into significant wealth at 22 and is now 36, putting him just inside Generation Y. Concerned that family money was not being spent in line with his own preferences, he joined Patriotic Millionaires for guidance on how to give his unearned wealth to good causes. His ancestors had concentrated on accumulating and preserving their fortune. Paolo prefers to redistribute it. This does not, however, prevent him from educating his children privately and enjoying nice holidays.

The article also features consultant Antonia Mitchell, founder of Aurelia Philanthropy, who helps clients give away money. Around 40% are aged under 40 and are keen to donate to causes such as supporting refugees, gender or race issues and problems affecting LGBTQ+ communities – matters that are often contentious, she says, between the generations.

* See below

Sources: Newspaper article cited; www.patrioticmillionaires.uk

Reparations

Organisations which promote philanthropic activism have multiplied in the UK as well as the US, albeit with a time-lag. One of the most prominent in Britain is the Beacon Collaborative. On its website is featured the story[21] of ex-BBC journalist Laura Trevelyan's voluntary payment of £100,000 for the educational benefit of the citizens of Grenada. This was triggered by revelations that her ancestors had amassed family wealth from slave-owning plantations in the Caribbean. The gift was formally pledged in a letter of 27 February 2023, whose co-signatories were six other fellow-descendants of the 18th century plantation owner Sir John Trevelyan, who also confirmed that they would donate educational bursaries.

The issue is one of the hottest of hot social activist potatoes, that of reparations: the demand that modern Western beneficiaries of the colonial era should both acknowledge and reimburse the descendants of those enslaved by their ancestors.

By no means were all of Sir John's 1,000 descendants in agreement with Laura. Among the counter-arguments, family members cited:

- that you can't apologise for an act that wasn't yours
- that it [payment of reparations] risked creating a potential "hornets' nest" of problems
- that what was effectively an admission of liability could open the family to legal action

- and that the family's reputation would be permanently tainted by association with slave-owning

Trevelyan herself admitted that her act had caused dissent, but her sense of inherited guilt and the need to make amends through reparation were stronger. Born in 1968, she is one of the oldest of the Generation X cohort. Britain's Prime Minister Sir Keir Starmer, on the other hand, has repeatedly rejected pressure from Caribbean countries to pay the enormous reparative sums demanded of Britain. Born in 1962, he is of the tail end of the Boomer generation.

Family Legacy and Sustainability

Less controversial, in the sense of minimising inter-generational tensions, are the correlations between a commitment to sustainability, a strong legacy and business performance uncovered by a study by the STEP[22] Project Consortium and KPMG Private Enterprise published in 2024.[23] The researchers surveyed 2,683 respondents across the globe and followed up with face-to-face interviews across generations in different regions. Their focus was primarily on defining and exploring *legacy* and what this meant in the context of family businesses. The report argues that legacy looks both forwards and backwards and has four dimensions: material [wealth], biological [successive generations], social [status in the community] and identity [who you are and what you stand for]. The significance of each dimension in contributing to a family's sense of legacy varies by culture, but what seems very clear is that *sustainability* is a highly useful glue for creating cohesion. As a concept, it has the great advantage of being both broad and subject to multiple interpretations. Since the start of this century, sustainability has emerged as an umbrella concept embracing business and ethical goals. For a business, it means fair, transparent, and socially responsible behaviour in all its dealings. Viewed through the lens of family business stewardship, it also implies the sustaining of a business into the indefinite future. As a philosophy, it is difficult to argue with, and meets both the ideals of a younger generation and the material requirements of the generation currently running the business or charged with overseeing the family's wealth.

The hallmark of sustainability has manifested itself in the last two decades through B-Corp certification, which first became available in 2007. Created by the American B – standing for Benefit – Lab, it was part of a growing social movement to encourage business as a force for good. At the start of 2025, 9,480 companies worldwide had successfully applied for and received certification: there are around 2,400 certified B Corporations in the UK. B-Lab certification recognises that accredited organisations voluntarily meet certain standards of transparency, accountability, sustainability, and performance, the aim being to create value for society, and not just for traditional stakeholders such as the shareholders. B-Lab is also unique in having a formal partnership with the United Nations to help the private sector translate its declared Sustainable Development Goals [SDG] into practical business processes.[24] Becoming a B-Corp is a protracted process, and a fairly expensive one that requires re-certification every three years. It takes both time and money.

What is the relevance to this book? First, though there are no precise data defining how many B-Corp businesses are family-owned or controlled, anecdotally, it seems that a good number are. Ground Control, for example, a UK commercial landscaping business owned and run by husband and wife Simon and Kim Morrish, gained B-Corp accreditation in the autumn of 2022. For this Generation X couple, it signalled their commitment to ethical goals to both their employees and their client base.

Second, affluent members of Generations Y and Z actively seek out brands which have B-Corp credentials, according to *The Great Wealth Transfer* report: a consumption trend which it terms "purposeful luxury." It is not enough for the watch, piece of jewellery, or garment to be attractive in its own right. The vendor must have acquired the raw materials ethically, manufactured the item responsibly and be able to demonstrate that it supports the right social causes. Among brands cited are Prada, Chloé [where Karl Lagerfeld and Stella McCartney were formerly artistic directors], and Cartier. Vestiaire Collective, which was founded to resell luxury fashion, and Gucci, now also in the business of reselling "pre-loved" items, are also mentioned, presumably for their buy-in to the circular economy.

It is digitisation, which dominates the world in which these generations have grown up, that has produced this blurring of the lines between luxury, art, culture and sustainability. A fascination with emergent technologies, such as blockchain[25] accounting, has led to the adoption of this approach by some of these brands. Where art is concerned, recent years have seen a flurry of interest in NFTs – non-fungible tokens – or fractional, digital "ownership" of a work of art that has been split, almost like a timeshare apartment, into multiple parts. Those participating in this market push the idea that NFTs in some way democratise the art market through enabling distributed ownership at reduced prices, and clearly believe that their NFTs are assets with value as long as other like-minded people are prepared to buy them.

And the Old Order Must Get with It

The Great Wealth Transfer report also describes the frustration younger affluent respondents feel with the current wealth management set-up, and the people who largely populate it. These managers are people who were appointed by the previous generation[s] and, unsurprisingly, tend to be of a similar age and background. Their mandate was the careful stewardship of the family's wealth, not for today or tomorrow but for the long haul. Their investment preferences [asset allocation, in the industry jargon] tend towards the traditional, with a preference for stocks, bonds, property, cash and so forth. Some among the new generation seem set on a collision course with people whom their parents trust and value, but whom they see as unsympathetic and out of touch with the modern world. The report cites research from CapGemini to the effect that only 18% of next-generation heirs are satisfied with their current wealth management adviser. Perhaps that dissatisfaction will mellow with age and a few burned fingers as the next great opportunity goes sour or ethical investing goes out of fashion. In the meantime, those younger family members who already enjoy wealth in their own right can choose to bypass intermediaries and make their own direct investments in the digital world they've embraced.

In Conclusion

Without doubt, a vast wave of inherited wealth will sweep across the world within the next two decades. A very significant proportion will take the form of money originating from family businesses.

This poses a number of big questions, both for those who inherit and for the governments of the countries in which the heirs to these fortunes reside and where those assets are held.

- In many instances, those leaving the legacies, such as the signatories to the Giving Pledge, have made their intentions very clear. Much of that wealth is to pass to philanthropic causes. Charitable legacies carry tax advantages for donors during their lifetimes, and for the estates they leave behind [although greater in the United States than in other jurisdictions]. Pledges to campaigns such as the Giving Pledge are not, however, legally binding and could be subject to challenge by heirs. Family disputes are as common between the very rich as the rest of us, and there will always be a few people who persist in believing that they have been hard done by. I have mentioned the bright future which awaits those in the ecosystem of family support, such as private banks, business schools, concierge service providers, consultancies and so forth. To their ranks we should perhaps add mediators and probate lawyers.
- Many families will, on the other hand, shun the publicity that a public row creates, and their members will prefer to make do with being rather less extremely rich. Those who are still troubled by the size of their good

fortune can seek help from organisations like The Beacon, which can connect them with advisors such as Iris Brilliant, a self-described anti-capitalist money coach "who helps wealthy people address any shame and anxiety they may have about their money."

- For the charities, museums and educational institutions which are the recipients of legacy gifts, a significant donation can be something of a mixed blessing. In Chapter 1, I highlighted the challenge of unravelling the Sackler donations faced by organisations such as the British Museum and the University of Oxford. Other future beneficiaries may well face similar problems when campaigning organisations confront them with unsavoury facts about the benefactions they receive.
- The different generations, as delineated in Figure 4.1 above, have been shaped by very different historical events, and their attitudes have been greatly influenced by new technologies. These factors impact their behaviour, especially when it comes to patterns of consumption and philanthropic initiatives. The evidence suggests that many among the rising generation, as they come into their inheritances, will wish to do things somewhat differently from their parents. Will that preference for social activism over what I have described as traditional philanthropy persist, or will their radicalism soften with the disenchantment that so often comes with age?
- Faced with this tide of affluence, governments will have to decide whether the new heirs are to be welcomed as friends providing new sources of investment and moderate tax revenues, or shunned as perpetrators of a widening social division and a source of greater wealth inequality, to be taxed as heavily as possible and their wealth redistributed. To judge from recent actions, most Western European governments are in two minds. A prominent member of the last Labour administration famously declared that it had no problem with people getting "filthy rich," provided they paid their taxes.[26] Under the current Labour government, a millionaire has allegedly been leaving British shores every 45 minutes. The most recent high-profile candidate widely rumoured to seek domicile elsewhere[27] is the Indian-born tycoon Lakshmi Mittal, Executive Chairman of his family's steel business Arcelor Mittal, and the eighth-richest person in the UK, worth almost £15 billion. As I have argued elsewhere, Mittal and his family are prime examples of global citizens who can choose to live more or less anywhere. Their tax position has been adversely affected by changes to the non-domiciled [non-dom] rules. Between them, the top 100 UK taxpayers – names such as Sir James Dyson, J.K. Rowling, the Duke of Westminster – pay around £5 billion in taxes, according to the most recent *Sunday Times* report.[28] [That, I should make clear, is their contribution in the single most recent tax year of record.] The snowball

effect also applies to taxes: tax liabilities tend to grow in line with a business's expansion. In the 60 years that Berkshire Hathaway has been in business, the firm has contributed a total of US$101 billion to the US government, the largest sum paid by any firm in history.[29]

Five of the top ten British taxpayers are described as families, four currently owning businesses and one that sold out in 2024. Fifty-seven of the top 100 are also families, either first- or multi-generational, the majority owning their own businesses. What will happen if they also decide to up sticks?

* * *

Notes

1 See www.legacyfutures.com: the same firm estimates that UK legacy and in-memory giving combined will double in real terms [inflation-adjusted] in the next 25 years.
2 According to the *Sunday Telegraph* on 11 May 2025, estimated charitable giving in the US amounted to US$557 bn, or £420 billion.
3 www.givingpledge.org: the pledge, it should be said, is a gesture of intent, not a legally binding contract.
4 www.wealthx.com/report/the-wealth-x-billionaire-census-2018/
5 LinkedIn news update, 17 January 2025.
6 See, for example, the *Financial Times* on Friday 10 January.
7 Reported in the *Financial Times* on Tuesday 14 January 2025.
8 Based on research published by Henley & Partners, the *Sunday Telegraph* on 19 January 2025 reported that over 10,000 US$ millionaires [people with net liquid assets exceeding roughly £821,000] left the UK in 2024, a number more than double that of 2023. Favoured destinations were Switzerland, the UAE, the US, and Singapore. *The Spectator* on 10 May 2025, pp. 10–11, covered the same topic, drawing on a broader evidence base, reaching similar conclusions.
9 The *Daily Telegraph* on Saturday, 25 January 2025, citing data from the UK's Office of National Statistics [ONS] reported that Boomer wealth, measured by total assets owned, exceeds that of Generation Z by 33 times.
10 Paralleled only by population surges from Latin America into the United States.
11 *Financial Times*, 24 January 2025.
12 As indicated in the Table above, it is too soon to comment on Generation Alpha.
13 LSE Centre for Economic Performance.
14 Institute for Fiscal Studies, Statista.
15 Available for download from www.modernaffluence.co.uk
16 Number 1 is the Danish Novo Nordisk foundation, and number 2, the Indian Tata Trusts: another family foundation.
17 Downloadable from www.altrata.com
18 UHNW individuals defined as those with assets above $US30 million: the Report estimated their number worldwide at a little short of 400,000.

19 A New Climate Movement? *Extinction Rebellion's Activists in Profile*. https://cusp.ac.uk/themes/p/xr-study/
20 See, for example, www.telegraph.co.uk/news/2023/05/26/chelsea-flower-show-protests-posh/ and www.spectator.co.uk/article/we-need-to-talk-about-just-stop-oils-class-privilege/
21 www.beaconcollaborative.org.uk/story/laura-trevelyan-i-hope-my-apology-and-reparations-for-my-familys-slave-owning-past-will-set-an-example-to-others/
22 Society of Trust and Estate Practitioners.
23 See https://kpmg.com/xx/en/our-insights/workforce/unlocking-legacy.html
24 *Business Insider*, 23 May 2019.
25 Blockchains are effectively distributed ledgers, recording transactions between different parties, these records – "blocks" of data – being encrypted. Advocates of corporate transparency favour this system because each record is date-stamped and cannot be altered or tampered with: any attempt to do so would cause changes across the block, as all transactions are intimately linked in the same data block.
26 Attributed to Peter [Lord] Mandelson and reported in the *Guardian* on Thursday 26 January 2012.
27 The *Daily Telegraph*, 28 March 2025.
28 The *Sunday Times*, 22 January 2025.
29 As reported by *Bloomberg*, 24 February 2025.

Further Reading

Inheritocracy: It's Time to Talk about the Bank of Mum and Dad, Kilby, Eliza, 2024, Biteback Publishing, reissued Penguin Books 2025.

Philanthropy: From Aristotle to Zuckerberg, Vallely, Paul, 2020, Bloomsbury Publishing.

Reparations: Slavery and the Tyranny of Imaginary Guilt, Biggar, Nigel, 2025, Forum.

Afterword

In this book, I have set out to answer the following set of questions:

- What is the significance of the family throughout history?
- Is there a formula for the inter-generational longevity and survival of the family business?
- How is family wealth preserved either in the form of a family business or a business family?
- What is the impact of family businesses on the global economy?
- What are the geographic shifts in the concentration of family wealth across the world?
- What is the network of support [the eco-system] on which wealthy families rely?
- And how do different generations see the world and their role as agents of change?

From my investigation, there is no doubt in my mind that the family remains absolutely central to the flourishing of society: to its prosperity, to its cultural vitality, and its social cohesion. Successive attempts to undermine it or dismantle it have failed, and the family as an economic and social unit has always rebounded. That is not to deny the obvious, that families can be deeply dysfunctional and mutually destructive. They are, after all, composed of people.

Across the world, inter-generational family-owned business survival rates, where they can be measured, exhibit, on average, the same pattern of steep decline over time. In some cases, the damage is self-inflicted, either because of feuding between siblings and cousins, or because there is no provision for both foreseeable and unforeseen eventualities such as divorce, remarriage or premature death. Occasionally, it happens, as in the case of Wilko, through poor judgement and what looks like simple greed. Like the legendary frog in a warming saucepan that cannot detect the progressive rise in water temperature

DOI: 10.4324/9781003685487-6

and fails to leap out before it boils to death, a family firm can succumb to incremental adverse changes unless it takes stock periodically. These days there are well-established processes and structures which skilled professionals can bring to bear to forestall such problems. On the other hand, the formula that has served the Rothschild dynasty so well over three centuries – large numbers of offspring, shrewd alliances, an ethos that allows family members to dip in and out of the business, and an openness to talented non-family members entering the firm in senior positions – appears to be an enduring template for a thriving legacy and may well apply equally in the future to modern clans such as the Arnaults.

At the same time, the shift of a family business into a business family, also a factor in declining inter-generational survival rates, is not always a bad thing. Not every succeeding generation wants to take over the reins, or is suited to do so. Like other enterprises, family businesses are subject to market dynamics, and merger or acquisition may make perfect strategic sense as the best means of preserving both the family's wealth and its cohesion. Family wealth also creates a wider choice of careers for the next generation, outside the family business, thus limiting the theoretical number of next-generation members available to work in the business. Preserving the accumulated wealth depends crucially on taking the long view, a willingness to defer short-term gratification, and allowing the snowball of compound interest to continue to roll. Infrequent cases like the Wilko collapse illustrate all too well the dangers of short-sightedness trumping careful stewardship: promoting individual enrichment to the detriment of the wider community.

The impact of family businesses on the global economy is without doubt significant. Virtually everywhere, such firms still form the backbone of national economies, forming the majority of small businesses. The evidence suggests that family businesses across the board have outperformed their non-family peers in recent years and that they are also more widely trusted by consumers. Where family businesses have transitioned – fully or partially – into business families, they release funds which, if wisely invested, fund economic growth and development. They also power good causes, locally, nationally, and across the world.

The geographic shifts in the concentration of family wealth in the last few decades are also exceptional. World economic history of the 19th and 20th centuries was shaped in very large part by the imperial European powers and by the United States, which was starting to supersede the British Empire as early as the last quarter of the 19th century. For most of the 20th century, American economic power was unchallenged and unchallengeable: the fall of the Soviet empire revealed the flimsiness of the Russian model and its satellites. The economic story of the 21st century so far can be summarised briefly as the extraordinary rise of China to challenge the supremacy of America, the growth of India hard on the heels of China, the ever-increasing prominence of the Arabian peninsula, and the slow decline of Europe. As an illustration:

- China is the world's largest exporter and has held that position since 2009
- the Tata dynasty from India owns both Jaguar/Land Rover and the UK's largest steel company, Tata Steel [the second-largest being controlled – until recently – by China's Jingye Group]
- Saudi Arabia will host the Football World Cup in 2034; Qatar has already done so in 2022. With virtually no sporting traditions to its name, Dubai and the UAE generally increasingly host major tournaments, in such sectors as golf, motor racing, tennis, and cricket, where the ruling families have effectively bought their way into sports followed by millions across the world.
- Europe lost its one true tech giant in the form of Britain's Cambridge-based Arm Holdings in 2014, when it was acquired by Japan's SoftBank for a price of £23.4 billion, or US$32 billion. The company was floated on the Nasdaq exchange in New York in September 2023, and is now valued at around US$120 billion. Though it still has a strong R&D base in Cambridge, it is run effectively from Palo Alto, California.
- Europe's most valuable enterprise today is luxury goods conglomerate LVMH, majority-owned by the Arnault family. It is anchored in the "old" economy. The most valuable *global* businesses are the US tech giants, pioneering innovation and entire new industries, and are decidedly not family businesses. Is this a portent of the future?

By way of consolation, two of Britain's most successful global manufacturing businesses, JCB and Dyson, are both privately-held and under family control. We will come back to the situation Europe finds itself in.

These shifts in global power and influence are reflected in the global listings of family businesses discussed in Chapter 2. North American dynasties are still dominant, and the old wealth of Europe clings on, but the ultra-rich clans of Asia-Pacific and South Asia are steadily climbing through the ranks.

* * *

In the first quarter of 2025, the world order as we had known it was subject to a seismic shock. On the 20th January, Donald Trump was inaugurated as the 47th President of the United States of America. From day one, he initiated the series of measures which he had promised to introduce in his election campaign. He had warned that he was going to shake things up, and he did. There is an old saying that politicians campaign in poetry, but govern in prose. Many, perhaps most, commentators expected that much of Trump's words were just empty rhetoric, a vague statement of intent, perhaps, not concrete policies. They were wrong. It may be that his proposals, such as annexing or purchasing Canada and Greenland, are laying the groundwork for negotiations in which the ultimate aim is less quasi-imperial expansion so much as maximising America's advantage by browbeating the parties on the other side of the table.[1] It's hard to know: even his close aides concede his unpredictability.

Trump's economic policies, in particular the imposition of swingeing tariffs on imports, run counter to the long-term global trend of progressive reductions in the barriers to free trade, as discussed in Chapter 2. The broad consensus among economists is that these reductions have boosted wealth and raised living standards: reversing them will cause short-term pain to exporters, difficulties for US producers such as factories that rely on imported components, and inflated prices for American consumers. Perhaps these policies are also a negotiating stance. In early April 2025, however, Trump enjoyed the worst domestic public opinion ratings of any incoming US President for nearly a quarter of a century. Be very, very careful what you wish for.

On the other hand, the epidemic of COVID-19 had already shaken the foundations of globalisation. The absence of products on supermarket shelves and the cessation of car assembly operations for lack of parts were just two of the more visible signs underscoring the fragility of international supply chains. The whole notion of everything, everywhere, whenever you – the Western consumer – want it, can no longer be taken as read. Perhaps some of what Trump has to say, especially regarding American isolationism, is actually the confirmation of some uncomfortable facts we have been reluctant to acknowledge.

At the time of writing these words, the major part of this book has been completed. Now, within a matter of weeks, the global economic [and political] order described in the previous pages has been upended: British Prime Minister Sir Keir Starmer recently stated, "The world as we knew it has gone."[2] Whether policies initiated by Trump are a blip, and "normality" will at some point return, or if they serve as the starting pistol for a new era, I frankly have no idea. Judging by the resulting confusion and general bewilderment around much of the world, I am unsure whether anyone else really knows. The new US President is a provocateur who cares little for conventional politics and even less about conventional wisdom. He has a grievance and a firm belief that America's huge budget deficit is the result of other countries exploiting the US, and can only be resolved by repatriating his nation's manufacturing industries: high import tariffs effectively hold a gun to the heads of US producers, especially the tech giants who have outsourced so much of their supply chains overseas. Foreign exporters to the US are also on notice. It is interesting that JCB, referred to above, has quickly reacted by announcing that it will double the size of its new plant in Texas[3] – a classic example of the agility of a great family-controlled business.

What is difficult to challenge, however, is that Trump is prepared to point out some hard truths. From a European perspective, the hardest of all to swallow is that the continent collectively has for decades spent too little on its own defence. Russia's invasion of Ukraine has brought this into sharp relief. Without American support of weaponry and intelligence, Ukraine would have been rapidly overrun. The collapse of the Soviet Union and the integration of large parts of Eastern Europe and the Baltic States into the western sphere diverted public spending from warfare to welfare, a shift accelerated by the COVID-19 crisis. Trump has made it clear that the NATO alliance can no longer expect to shelter under American largesse. In response, European leaders like Prime Minister Starmer have been falling over themselves in the rush to increase spending on defence.

Raising expenditure on defence implies greater investment in the technologies that underpin new developments. That may help to mitigate any trade wars. As *Bloomberg*'s Weekend Edition on 16 March 2025 argues, drawing from the work of LSE economist Ethan Ilzetski, a one per cent increase in defence spending may well translate into a 0.25% rise in productivity, with spillovers into the civilian economy. People learn simply by doing. Either way, it seems we have little choice: the post-war peace dividend has been spent.

What Does the Change in the Landscape Mean for the Globally Wealthy and Their Families?

Investment

First, in the immediate term, asset managers and Family Office professionals are likely at this moment rebalancing their investment portfolios, with a greater exposure to prime defence contractors and those companies that supply them.[4] In the short and medium term, within Europe there may well be a flurry of cross-border consolidation. National governments have tended to procure materiel from their own domestic defence industry champions – the British from British Aerospace and Babcock, for example, the French from Dassault and Thales, the Germans from Rheinmetall[5] and Krauss-Maffei Wegmann – which limits economies of scale and creates problems of "interoperability."[6] Throughout 2024 magazine *Family Capital* covered reports of Family Offices stepping up their engagement in merger and acquisition deals. It is not hard to foresee military procurement switching more towards a pan-European basis. At the same time, industrial innovation is often driven by new market entrants. Now may be a propitious time for family wealth to find its way into the increased co-financing of promising technology start-ups and fast-growth ventures.[7]

The Changing Role of the State

Second, the new mood music has forced a rethink of the role of the state. In the British post-war settlement, the notion of the welfare state was widely endorsed. It has dominated the political status quo in much of the rest of Europe. That consensus is clearly now in question. The most notable feature of European Union politics in 2024 was the rise of parties of the right, such as the National Rally in France, Alternative for Germany, Brothers of Italy, and the Netherlands Party of Freedom. In Britain, we have the Reform Party, which at the time of writing leads its mainstream rivals in national polling. These began as protest groups on the margins. Now they are in parliaments, if not actually in government. All share the aim of moderating, redirecting and to a degree curtailing the role and power of the state and the super-state, in the form of the European Union.

Until the banking crisis of 2007–2008 the ever-rising demands on the public purse of the welfare state model was a circle that could be squared by a healthy rate of economic growth. Borrow now, pay later. Governments behaved very much like someone who racks up credit in year one, secure in the knowledge of a salary rise in year two – and rather than paying off the accrued debt in the second year, rolls it forward, and frequently adds to it in the expectation of a further salary rise in year three. [In the UK, even this stratagem had to be augmented by "off-balance sheet" financing ruses, like the Private Financing Initiatives [PFI schemes] introduced by the last Labour government, which funded construction of schools and hospitals.] This approach, however, depends crucially on a robust rate of increase in GDP, and the continuing willingness of others, in many cases overseas financial institutions, to lend. It is also greatly assisted by very low rates of interest. All these factors were in play until they weren't. Foreign lenders still continue to buy UK government bonds, of course, but at a premium that reflects much higher central bank rates of interest and the perception of the UK as a less-than-stellar credit risk. The costs of servicing British national debt are currently over double the amount spent on defence. If you keep going back to your bank manager for an increase in your overdraft when your salary is more or less static, and your prospects are mediocre, don't be surprised if borrowing money gets ever more expensive. At some point, this has to stop.

Not just the UK, but other European countries carrying heavy burdens of indebtedness are facing the same existential question: what is the role of the state? Can it continue as before, or should it retrench to only core functions such as defence, security, education, health and a basic safety net for the poorest? With borrowing ever more expensive, the alternative is to raise taxes still further, a choice always open to the party in government, but which dramatically reduces the chances of re-election. If you are seeking to reinvigorate an economy, pouring ever more money into the public sector without major reform seems a curious way to go about it.

Where the wealthy are concerned, there seem to be two implications. In straitened times, the rational course of action for governments is to make residency for the rich as attractive as possible.[8] As I have already cited, a number of countries are creating incentives to attract wealthy retirees and those with money to invest. There will be competition between nations and a growing tendency for a buyer's market in residency for taxation purposes to emerge, though traditional tax havens like Monaco, Lichtenstein and Switzerland can probably afford to raise the bar for entry. For the *really* rich, a battery of lawyers and accountants can be relied on to secure the most attractive arrangements. In covering the global mobility of billionaires, UBS [the Union Bank of Switzerland] reported net movements[9] in early 2025 as follows:

Net inflows:

- 20 into Western Europe
- 13 into North America
- 8 into the Middle East/North Africa
- 25 into China

Net outflows:

- 9 from Central/South America
- 29 from Eastern Europe
- 8 from Southeast Asia
- 6 from Oceania

This pattern implies a liking for comparative political stability, a certain type of lifestyle, and perceived business opportunities. Who knows what future actions on the part of the Trump administration may affect the geographic preferences of the ultra-wealthy?[10]

In Britain, the attitude of the present government towards family business seems decidedly ambivalent. Until now, the qualifying assets held by family businesses were subject to 100% tax relief. Changes announced to inheritance tax and business property relief as of April 2026 will alter the picture dramatically. The relief on qualifying assets will be cut to 50%, and those inheriting business assets will be charged a levy of 20% on assets valued at over £1 million.[11] The plight of smaller family farms, asset-rich but cash-poor, has received the widest coverage, but the new fiscal regime will affect a large number of family-owned businesses across the board. Is the UK government's aim primarily to plug a short-term gap in the public finances, or is it a longer-term project designed to use increased taxation as a mechanism for the redistribution of wealth? Whatever the motive, the law of unintended consequences lurks on the sidelines. The *Daily Telegraph* on 30 August 2025 featured the case of Steve Perez, founder of drinks manufacturer Global Brands Ltd and employer of 400 people in the former mining town of Chesterfield, in Derbyshire. If the business passes to the next generation, it will cost his heirs £7 million in tax. The alternative, the sale to a large corporation, will likely lead to the loss of all or a large number of those 400 jobs in an area with limited employment alternatives. Either way, says Perez, his family will manage, but he has been advised that the best course of action is for him to leave the country. He intends to stay and weather the storm, but is the government's approach really in the national interest? Does it want to encourage family businesses or not?

Philanthropy

A further implication is that if governments *do* retrench to their core functions, then wealthy families are likely to feel an even greater sense of obligation to take up the slack where philanthropy is concerned. The vast projected flows to charity that result from inheritances may prove to be an underestimate. Reacting to Trump's call to European leaders to raise their defence spending, from 2027 the British government will cut the annual overseas development budget from 0.5% of GDP to 0.3% [the previous Conservative administration had already reduced it from 0.7% of GDP in 2020]. This is just one example. Overseas aid expenditure is invisible to most people. People will truly feel the pinch when state spending on domestic matters is tightened. If the state wishes to promote giving to good causes, then the logical course of action is to harness the existing tendencies of wealthy families towards philanthropy and incentivise them to do more by changing the tax system in their favour. As the journalist Michael Mosbacher points out in the *Sunday Telegraph* on 11 May 2025, US tax rules governing philanthropic giving are not so much more generous as simply less complex than the UK equivalent. Comparatively speaking, US taxpayers are more than four times as magnanimous in their giving as the British. The gap could be narrowed just by encouraging more families to establish Family Charitable Trusts, which are both tax-efficient and ensure that giving reaches the intended beneficiaries: the

Weston family's Garfield Weston Foundation, to take but one example, distributes about £100 million every year.

No doubt this will be greeted by protests against tax breaks for the rich, but there may be little alternative if the state is focused on redirecting public money towards its basic obligations. Do the residents of a Peabody estate or a Guinness Partnership, as it now is, really care that the roofs over their heads were originally provided by a 19th-century philanthropist? Or do the patients treated by the new Cancer centre at Bath's Royal United Hospital concern themselves that it was funded by the generosity of the Dyson family?

* * *

And what of our fictional family, described in Chapter 3? What does the future hold for the second generation, the sibling partnership, still actively managing the company which their parents created? And will their children, the next generation, step up to form a cousin consortium to take the business forward through the 21st century?

My crystal ball is opaque. Perhaps an offer will be made that is simply too good to refuse, and this family business will be transformed into a business family, whose wealth is no longer largely bound up in a single asset base. At any rate, the third generation will have to navigate a world where the old certainties no longer apply and agility is essential to the preservation of wealth. They will, however, benefit greatly from the eco-system that has accrued in the last few decades to support and sustain families of means, the network of wealth managers, advisors, consultants and other professionals. If this generation is wise, they will ensure that long-term family harmony prevails over whatever disputes and disagreements may arise between them. If they are of a generous heart and spirit, they will see that great wealth carries great obligations and will use their inheritance also to benefit others less fortunate than themselves.

But I can make one prediction with some certainty. Regardless of circumstances, family businesses and business families are set to continue as the backbone of economic growth and well-being. They deserve our support.

Notes

1 A number of Trump's inner circle, including Elon Musk, have reacted by pressing hard for free trade zones, such as zero-tariffs between the US and Europe: *Bloomberg* Bulletin, 7 April 2025. Perhaps that is the end-game?
2 Reported in the *Daily Telegraph* on 5 April 2025.
3 *Construction Enquirer*, www.constructionenquirer.com/2025/04/03/jcb-to-double-size-of-us-factory-in-wake-of-trump-tariffs/

4 On 20 March 2025 market intelligence firm Beauhurst released reports on the ramping-up of activity by leading British and German defence firms. See *UK Defence Tech* and the blog feature on German defence companies at www.beauhu rst.com
5 According to the *Financial Times* on 13 March, the company is scouring Germany for extra capacity to produce tanks, one candidate being Volkswagen's dormant car factories.
6 One nation's armed forces cannot use the weapons produced by another country
7 The UK's own recent start-up Cambridge Aerospace, founded to build low-cost drone interceptors, is a good example of a private equity-backed business looking to scale up rapidly.
8 HMRC's own figures show that 1% of British taxpayers, the highest earners, contribute almost 30% of income tax: source House of Common Library. According to the Adam Smith Institute, it is the Treasury's largest source of revenue.
9 The 2024 UBS Billionaire Ambitions report states that between 2020 and April 2024, of 2,682 global billionaires identified, 176 had relocated.
10 Free market think-tank the Adam Smith Institute tracks the net exodus of millionaires from the UK: see www.adamsmith.org/millionaire-tracker2024
11 Subsequently revised to £2.5 million on 23 December 2025.

Index